To
Margaret
With Best Wishes
John Daly

Windmills of the Mind

A Collection of Poems by John Daly

An INSPIRE.ie Production
SKIBBEREEN, CO. CORK, IRELAND

Contents

Introduction

Emerson once wrote 'the only true gift is a portion of yourself'. With this in mind I offer these, my poems, rough and ragged and simple, though they may be.

And although the themes may be worn threadbare with overuse, they still stir my soul to song when I walk through the dream-haunted meadows of memory.

They were written in the myriad moods that make me who I am, and probably say more about me than I would care to admit.

If you hope to find great classical poetry here, I fear you will be disappointed. All are simple rhymes that may touch a chord in the heart, and transport you down the ribbon roads of remembrance.

Windmills of the Mind

You are with me in the misty white of morning,
When I walk the leafy lanes of long ago,
As the velvet-footed years with scarce a warning,
On the turbulent tides of time did onward flow.

Let the future keep it's secrets and it's silence,
In dawn's delights I did not want to know,
As hand in hand we walked in springtime's gardens,
And fairer than the flowers I watched you grow.

Winter marked me while you sipped the wines of summer,
And beneath your canopy of curls did beauty glow,
And your loveliness outshone the bright star's glimmer,
As the pendulum of time swung to and fro.

Now I am jealous of strange people and strange places,
That see you bloom and blossom like a rose,
As other scenes and other sights your heart embraces,
While the sails of dream's old windmills seek repose.

In the petal painted portals of the morning,
Hand in hand we walk again among the flowers,
But it's just a fantasy within my heart sojourning,
Since you've grown I count the footfalls of the hours.

After All

My life has overflowed the cup,
Of love and friendship through the years,
In sorrow too I've had to sup,
The dismal dregs of bitter tears.

When death will come to call for me,
Uncomplaining I will take his hand,
And shirking not his company,
I'll step into his shadowed land.

And sing no sad songs over me,
Those sombre chants I could not bear,
The singing breezes from the sea,
Are the only hymns my soul shall hear.

There are faithful friends who will walk with me,
Beyond the last mile marking stone,
To the grave's dark door keep me company,
From there I must journey on alone.

And place no blossoms on the mound,
Where they would wither and decay,
But roses of remembrance round,
Me scatter, when I go away.

There are fond hearts who will weep for me,
Who have loved me more than I could know,
Please do not grieve, I'll wait for ye,
Along the road we each must go.

Betrayal

Let others dream where I have cried,
Let others sleep untroubled,
Let others turn their eyes away,
Lest they see something they shouldn't.

They might have seen what I have seen,
And be haunted by it's horror,
The helplessness; and the hopelessness,
And the torment; and the terror.

Poor frightened children in the dark,
In whose hearts fear nightly festers,
Lest the footsteps stop beside their bed,
With hoarse and urgent whispers.

Who are you that took the vows,
To follow the good Lord's teaching?
Instead you gratified your lust,
And sneered at a child's beseeching.

You betrayed the Saviour's gentle creed,
When he gathered the children round him,
You drove the nails in his hands and feet,
And with twisted thorns you crowned him.

And you betrayed good men of God,
Good men who were your betters,
And tarred them all with the same black brush,
And shackled them with shame's foul fetters.

Still they call to us from the rock-strewn road,
With the kind words of the Saviour,
As they try to right the wrongs you've done,
By your depraved behaviour.

Those who sheltered you from the eyes of man,
They too; to their God must answer,
Their guilt was just as great as yours,
In perpetrating this fetid cancer.

Echoes

The echoes of unwritten songs,
Now faint and fainter grow.
But the music hangs in the haunted air,
Though the words have ceased to flow.

And the radiant rose of ardent dreams,
Has withered and decayed.
Still it's fragrance oft frequents the dark,
When slumber is delayed.

Could I capture yet again perchance,
These mystic melodies,
And the eloquence of vibrant verse,
That whispers in the breeze?

When I would see a brimming brook,
Whose banks the fern-fronds throng,
I'd snare it's soul in a web of words,
And weave it in a song.

Now thoughts turn back on cogs of pain,
When evening zephyrs weep.
As I rest awhile my weary wings,
And solace find in sleep.

A captive of the creeping years,
My songs I'll sing no more.
The pen hangs idle from my hand,
Blank pages strew the floor.

Soul-Mates

Dame Fortune lavished love's great gifts on me,
Beyond the wildest wishes of my mind,
When love's arrow pierced two hearts with ecstasy,
Two soul-mates throbbing heartbeats intertwined.

Unresisting I've been forged upon love's fires,
And love's anvil shaped the dreams of yearning years,
You fan to flame my passions and desires,
And lure to laughter all my lonely tears.

Love's sensuous seraph in rapture round me sings,
His sweetness serenades me night and day,
Within my heart he folds his fragile wings,
And will here within my heart forever stay.

A Hundred Years From Now

When I have laid my dreams aside,
With the laughter of unclouded years,
And death casts adrift on the ebbing tide,
All my trials and tears.

May I have time to make amends,
For the wrongs I might have done,
As my prayers to Heaven's Gate ascents,
Before my race is run.

I may have hurt a thousand hearts,
I may have harmed but one,
I pray 'ere life from me departs,
I still can say t'were none.

May I look back with no regret,
May doubt not dim my days,
And when I draw my final breath,
May I on God's glory gaze.

To your best aspire, though bent with age,
If time's thief the days allow,
It's legacy will paint the page,
A hundred years from now.

Where Beauty Kneels

I watch the starry flowers with wonder,
Blossom in the evening sky,
And I hear the talking thunder,
And the west winds softly sigh.

And I'm enchanted by sweet bird-song,
In misty morning mountain airs,
And stealthy shadows, stepping one by one,
Down the Comeragh's stony stairs.

The tides of thought that drench my dreams,
And flood imagination's strand,
Conjure up strange sights and scenes,
And castles built on shifting sand.

But I have no wish to wander far,
Or around this wondrous world to roam,
I can see from here the farthest star,
And never venture from my home.

But think you not that I am poor,
With but idleness my days to fill,
When welcome's wealth adorns my door,
And rainbow's gold gleams on the hill.

Until the grinding mills of pain,
Crush my days between their wheels,
I'll hoard the harvest's golden grain,
I reaped in rhyme, where beauty kneels.

Whispers In The Wind

Whisper ye breezes a message to me,
Where are ye going or have been?
Ye that have travelled o'er land and o'er sea,
Tell of all the strange sights ye have seen.

Did ye move o'er the mountains that touch the blue sky?
Did ye dance in the deepest ravine?
Did ye hear as ye passed the lost lover's sigh,
Or see the tear that no other has seen?

Did ye see heavy hearts in lands far away?
Did ye see faces dumb with despair?
Did ye see homeless hordes with no place to stay,
Bewildered by a world that won't care?

Did ye hear a soft splash in the swift ebbing tide,
As another soul ceases to fight?
Did ye see the mantle of hope cast forever aside?
Did ye touch a life lost in the night?

Did ye see the bright smile of the innocent and pure,
Crushed under the jack-boot of crime?
And dreams born in the dawn that were meant to endure,
But were strangled by the slip-knot of time.

Did ye see the light linger at the coming of night?
Did ye hear a voice wail in the wind?
Did ye hear heaven lament in the last of the light,
As again and again we have sinned?

A Dream Within A Dream

To the passive peace and quiet of lonely places,
And hushed solitude and silence I belong,
There I see again the old familiar faces,
That in a dream within a dream around me throng.

In the silence stretch the shadows of the ages,
And dim the days that softly came and went,
Inexorably are turned times tattered pages,
That will close the book of life, so briefly lent.

But why lament the time I may have squandered?
Or see only storm-tossed clouds across the moon,
And if sometimes from the well-worn path I wandered,
From the darkest night the dawn will follow soon.

And dawn will call the birds to serenade me,
And the rising sun will chase the chill away,
And contentment will upon me settle softly,
And the sunset will bring peace at close of day.

Then other hands will pluck the flowers I planted,
And their perfume will pervade the evening air,
Beyond the zenith of the years that I was granted,
May love and hope and laughter linger there.

Is There Someplace?

Is there some place; some peaceful place,
Where the boats come always home?
Where no-one waits upon the quay,
Heart-broken and forlorn.

Where children's wishes are fulfilled,
Where wives need never weep,
Where the fishing boats at sunset,
Around homely headlands sweep.

Where the "holds" are always heavy,
Where the fishing's always fair,
And the terrors of the tempest,
Forever shouts elsewhere.

Where laps the shore a quiet tide,
When evening sails are due,
And peace pervades the twilights's fall,
And every dream comes true.

"O great good God!" if such there be,
Our broken hearts implore,
On the turning tide, our loved ones meet,
Who were drowned by green Glandore.

Jealousy

Across misty moonlit meadows we oft meandered,
Where star-silvered weeping willows vaguely gleam,
Love's sensuous secrets tenderly we plundered,
In the sighing stillness by a slumbering stream.

In swirling snows I saw flowers bloom and blossom,
In the tempest roar I heard the skylarks sing,
When love's garlands round my fervent heart you fashioned,
And winter wore the colours of the spring.

But a rose confined within a closed book's pages,
Soon in darkness will it's radiance cease to glow,
Though well beloved, it will wither with the ages,
And more pale with passing time it's petals grow.

In true love's throes is Trust: a jewel to cherish,
But I ringed your love with jealousy's sharpened spears,
And forgot the bird imprisoned will soonest perish,
Now the weary winds of time won't dry my tears.

The fault is mine the ties of love did sever,
And to the wild winds scattered true love's bright bouquets,
I was a slave to jealousy's green-eyed monster,
Now the gaunt ghosts of our love haunt all my days.

If Only We Had Known

To reach out a hand to a faltering friend,
Is a beautiful thing to do.
When he's down on his luck, but he knows full well,
He can always depend on you.
When the world from him turns it's face away,
And from pillar to post he's blown.
And you say you'd have helped him to rise again,
If only; you had known.

There's a pallid-faced urchin who begs through the town,
A mite for a meal he'll implore.
As you hurry on by you'll realise with a sigh,
You've seen him standing there often before.
If you thought for a moment that the hunger prowled,
Around the hovel that he called home.
You'd have emptied your purse, to help him along.
If only; you had known.

There are loved ones whose hearts are twined around yours,
And who look up to you as their light.
But who sometimes walk in a "Gethsemene" of grief,
Yet you note not how dark is their night.
You would willingly shoulder their burden of pain,
Their happiness means more than your own,
To their side you would hasten with a loving embrace,
If only; you had known.

But don't be downhearted; we are all much the same,
And now we wonder how we were so blind.
That we never could see what was plainly in view,
Were we selfish, uncaring, unkind?
We can still make amends and rekindle the past,
As when love's first spring blossoms blew.
"If only we'd known!" say never again,
For we knew; we knew; we knew;

Light And Dark

To be born in pain is life's cruel way,
To temper us for the years to be,
Love walks with loss down every day,
Light duels with darkness constantly.

Life's lamp is lit from the spark of love,
That in the dark will brightly flare,
It's secret whispered from above,
Is a gift from God for us to share.

And if your heart grows pale with pain,
Remember that this too will pass,
Though the taste of winter's wines remain,
When we drain the dregs from summer's glass.

As a pallid moon transforms the tide,
With flashing sparks of silver fire,
The stygian dark is shoved aside,
By hopes, and dreams and heart's desire.

And if we strive to grasp the sun,
Or to reach beyond the farthest star,
Know there's light enough for everyone,
To gain their goals; though they be far.

On Wayward Wings

At midnight's hour in vain I search,
For words and ways my tales to tell,
But I cannot grasp what I cannot reach,
In the gloom where rhymes no longer dwell.

They gambolled in the golden air,
When evening came to claim the day,
I could feel their fingers in my hair,
While they whispered things I wished to say.

When my pen perused the passive page,
And spun a web of silken words,
They sang the songs of youth and age,
Of love and loss and singing birds.

Then on wayward wings they went away,
Away; as though they never were,
But when darkness shuts the doors of day,
Vague voices whisper from afar.

If I could lure them back again,
Like silver streams my thoughts would flow,
Where old songs abide, and old dreams remain,
And rhymes like roses again would grow.

Solitude And Silence

As the skylark soars among the clouds domain,
In ecstasies of misty morning dew,
And the whispering waves down the shore complain,
Let me drift down daydream's paths and peace pursue.

When the sun has climbed across the gates of noon,
Give me leave to converse with one true friend,
And none call me to task, either late or soon,
Time's abundance will be measured at the end.

In a world more gentle than I ever knew,
Let me shed the strangling shackles of the mind,
And acquaintance with my soul once more renew,
And the innocence I lost again to find.

One hour of quiet content is all I seek,
In a weary world of sordid strife and care,
When evening's fingers search the shadows deep,
For the solitude and silence hidden there.

The Cynic

I would wish to be as I have been,
When love and trust were all I knew,
And deceitful smirks were never seen,
Behind the smiles I thought were true.

When everyone was a welcome friend,
And the world was a wondrous place to be,
Where every path was flower-fringed,
And every flower bloomed for me.

From these sweet wisps of memory,
I weave again a childhood dream,
That leaps to life in ecstasy.
When things are once more what they seem.

But some vague where, at some vague time,
Experience sowed a seed of doubt,
Too small I thought, to undermine,
The things a child might dream about.

Small it was in the world's great schemes,
When innocence abandoned me,
But the cynics curse destroyed my dreams,
Since the seed of doubt grew to a tree.

Childhood virtues are now crushed,
Beneath the harsh heel of the world,
And innocence; and dreams; and trust;
Upon life's rubbish heap are hurled.

Souls Of The Sea

When tired of tears and laughter,
And weary of well-worn ways,
Let us lift once more the anchor,
And sail back to distant days.

Passing years still paint reflections,
Where a lingering sunset gleams,
On the wrecks of fond affections,
In the harbours of our dreams.

Where the soul of a sailor surges,
To the ocean's oratory,
And rhymes of rain and wind converges,
In a storm-strummed symphony.

Sorrow weeps when a heart remembers,
As we pray for the souls of the sea,
How the fires of life dimmed to embers,
On the tall ships of memory.

Beyond where Helvick's regal ridges,
Sentinel the whispering waves,
And the sea croons grief's ghostly dirges,
Above the lonely ocean graves.

Bestow Lord! the gift of your favours,
This day of pageantry and prayer,
On Dungarvan boats and sailors,
Those here; and those out there.

Kneel with us at the ocean's altars,
Is our heartfelt cry to thee,
You who stilled the storm-troubled waters,
On the Sea of Galilee.

You

You leave love's footprints on my heart,
As if on crystal virgin snow,
But if you would from me depart,
From the ruined realms of life I'd go.

Where ere you are I know you're near,
When days across the swift years climb,
If distance makes the heart more dear,
Then it closer binds your soul to mine.

When you walk with me in the evening air,
Among the gardens ghostly gloam,
Your whispered words weave a silken snare,
That captures every breath I own.

The past; the present; the yet to be;
Across the tides of time endures,
Two fervent hearts one heart now be,
My life: my love; my world is yours.

You are the bridge that spans the tide,
And shepherds me to a sheltered shore,
Your shining star my footsteps guide,
Where you lead I'll follow evermore.

You shelter me from every storm,
You chase my faceless fears away,
Your cloak of love will keep me warm,
Till angel's wings about me play.

Mystic Music

Have you heard it in your dreaming?
Mystic music from the past,
Drifting down deserted beaches,
Like distant hoof-beats that have passed.

When there's a rapture in the stillness,
And evening spreads it's cloak,
Of silence 'round the twilight,
And sea-mist drifts in like smoke.

And the saffron stains have faded,
From the skyline in the west,
And the dusk turns day's dim pages,
And folding wings fill every nest.

When your eyes are growing drowsy,
And your thoughts begin to stray,
Gleams again the faded colours,
That you painted yesterday.

'Tis then you'll hear the mystic music,
Drifting ghost-like through the gloom,
And the roses of remembrance,
Will once more around you bloom.

Resurrection

The world laments the dying day,
And mournful winds are weeping.
The sun has stowed its lamps away,
And behind the hill is sleeping.

Silent now is the blackbird's song,
She hangs her head in sorrow.
Today she did not sing for long,
And may not sing at all tomorrow.

The moon still hides its frightened face,
And the world is shadow shaded.
As clouds across the grey skies race,
And evening's light has faded.

Days grow short, now summer's spent,
The swallows have departed.
With whistling wings away they went,
And leaves us heavyhearted.

But we might find one radiant ray,
Among cold embers sleeping.
If we re-live one summer's day,
When the world is wet with weeping.

In God's good time the earth will turn,
As it's done for years unnumbered,
And the summer sun will rise and burn,
From where it long has slumbered.

A Nation And A Name

I must go beyond the oceans, tormented by emotions,
Of loneliness and longing and a yearning to remain,
Round my feet in fragments shattered,
my dreams and hopes are scattered,
And my lovely land of Ireland will no more be the same.

When the pen of future sages, recount on history's pages,
How faithfully we followed the self-serving masquerade,
Of the fools who lured and led us and on greed's high altar bled us,
Until poverty plagued the passive, and the brave became afraid.

The bright blooms of hope we cherished in penury have perished,
And our distinguished heritage was wasted on the wind,
For thirty paltry bits of silver they have steered us to disaster,
On the shores of desolation the light of sovereignty was dimmed.

Is there no-one left to save us, as they continue to enslave us,
With false promises and lying rhetoric, for which they deny the blame?
How we miss those men of honour,
who fought 'neath freedom's banner,
And died in a hail of bullets; for a nation and a name.

After The Storm

The cliffs in the darkness are shrouded,
That soar high above Helvick's wild waves,
Like tombstones together they're crowded,
Keeping watch o'er a hundred ship's graves.
Out there where the swift surging ocean,
Sweeps the sea-wrack far up on the shore,
With the broom of it's incessant motion,
From the tide's rock-strewn weed-tangled floor.

In the depths by the dim sunken ledges,
Where a thousand lost seafarers sleep,
The pale moon from its slumber emerges,
To count the hours of the vigil they keep.
Memory weeps round their last resting places,
From Bunmahon's Copper Coast to Ardmore,
We still treasure those lost loving faces,
That only live now in legend and lore.

When the sky is by tempests tormented,
And the whirlwind is troubling the sea,
And the voice of the gale is demented,
In celestial wild oratory.
We'll batten down hard all the hatches,
And every halyard make fast to the cleat,
And in that wilderness of waves stand our watches,
O'er the graves of the sailors beneath.

'Tis likewise through the storms of existence,
We must strive though the odds are unfair,
When hope reaches far into the distance,
Contentment is somewhere out there.
And when evening is tinting the ocean,
And you've struggled through life without harm,
Thank God for your cup and your portion,
Always after the storm comes a calm.

Home For Christmas

Praise God! I'm on the last long mile from home,
In the passive peace of a half-moon's shadowed light,
A single star spills silver on the gloam,
But pregnant clouds make darker far the night.

But I care not if the night is black as coal,
As the freezing frost upon my shoulders fall,
Every bend along the bohereen I remember as of old,
And the face of every old friend I recall.

I've grown old since last I strolled through glebe and glen,
Before fickle fortune bestowed her smiles on me,
Gold weighs heavier in my pocket now than then,
But far sweeter was the old life than I knew it then to be.

I vowed I would return at Christmas time,
When the holly lamps were lit in lanes of green,
And the hungry grass is spear-like with frost rime,
Since the star I follow filled my every dream.

For old neighbours now time's sands have ceased to run,
And round dream haunted hearths the dead leaves play,
But this Christmas night, Thank God! I'm with my own,
Among the fields where my forefathers lay.

I Remember! I Remember!

We walked abroad at twilight,
'Ere April's suns had set,
Do you remember, darling?
Or perhaps, do you forget?

Love weaved it's webs in winter,
We were captives in the spring,
Like larks, we soared in summer,
On passions pulsating wing.

But when leaves were drifting downward,
Like rains of russet gold,
Autumn lit it's fragrant fires,
But love's fires had grown ash cold.

And elusive among the embers,
The ghost of a lost love lay,
And the roses left ungathered,
All withered to decay.

Blue skies turned black as thunder,
And the days to dusk have sunk,
But I remember; I remember;
Love's sweetest wine I've drunk.

Now in this place of shadows,
I will never weep again,
The well of tears is empty,
The grief too deep for pain.

Helvick

Ballinacourty's flashing beacon,
Is twilight's grey fields reaping,
As the evening piles about me,
The shadowed sheaves of night,
The turbulent tide is troubled,
And the waves are shoreward sweeping,
And to the sea-scourged cliffs of Helvick,
The lighthouse hurls it's spears of light.

The storm's splendour makes me sombre,
As recollection's spool unravels,
And it's trailing threads are tangled,
In the remnants of regret.
Dreams died and were discarded,
On the lost shores of my travels,
And of the radiant hopes extinguished,
'Twould be better to forget.

Fifty fragrant Junes have flowered,
And fifty verdant springs have vanished,
Since the withered leaves of boyhood,
Went swirling down life's lane.
From the fortune that I strived for,
Fate decreed that I be banished,
And fifty years were variegated,
By brush-strokes of peace and pain.

I had often heard the legend,
That a golden kingdom glimmered,
With gleaming towers and turrets,
Like an ancient Babylon,
Beyond the homely hills of Helvick,
On the rose-red seas that shimmered,
Out beyond the far horizon,
At the setting of the sun.

To World's End I wandered westward,
To find the Kingdom of the Sunset,
But I was lured by an illusion,
That had held my heart in thrall,
But tonight at last I've found it,
In tranquil silhouette I see it,
My paradise beyond the rainbow,
My rose beyond recall.

I can see now through the tempest,
In the grey ghost of the twilight,
What enchanted me in childhood,
Fifty wasted years ago,
The paradise I searched for,
Is shining in the shadowed moonlight,
Helvick is my Golden Kingdom,
But I was then too blind to know.

Silent Scream

Must solitude forever be my lot?
In the teeming throng must I always feel alone?
Around the lamp of life, am I a timid moth,
That barely touched the light; then away had flown?

A pale, gaunt ghost inhabits passion's place,
Where the fires of love should be burning fiercely bright,
But cold embers in the hearth the flames replace,
And the petals fall 'ere the bud blooms in the light.

With malaise of mind and melancholy heart,
I hide my face from the crowded haunts of men,
And find solace in the shadowed place apart,
Where their indifference is no dagger to me then.

Long have I heard rejection's silent scream,
That insidiously re-echoes down the years,
It's as strident now as 'ere before has been,
And it fills my days with vague unfounded fears.

If I could stand on a morning mountain peak,
Where my troubled soul could soar in lost delight,
And find at last the gentler world I seek,
And with and eagle's freedom spread my wings in flight.

The Fallen Tree

You have stood there for three hundred years or more,
Where one small road in divergent ways did sever,
I thought as I passed that way 'oft times before,
You would stand in solitary splendour there forever.

When springtime in your verdure stirred again,
And the west wind ran it's fingers through your hair,
You raised strong arms to embrace soft April rain,
And to welcome raucous rooks nestbuilding there.

Jim Power's patient horse would drowse and dream,
In the coolness of your whispering colonnade,
While around your roots the playful passing stream,
Shyly sang it's ceaseless serenade.

At evening, men would gather in your shade,
And talk of things long gone; or things to come,
You have seen in those dim twilights, life's parade,
And with the passing of the years, mourned sire and son.

You'll nod your wise old head now nevermore,
Or see the rising and receding of the sea,
Or listen to the sibilant wet-lipped lore,
Of the stream that tumbles towards the "Barrnawee".

From a seedling for three hundred years you've grown,
But the woodman in three minutes threw you down,
To "Cloncoskerine's" green groves the rooks have flown,
And you lie dead and broken on the ground.

The Rendezvous

Death's dismal dirges around me flow,
Love! Hold me close; then let me go,
When my last breath he steals from me,
I will love you then, for eternity.

While yet tis cruel and hardly fair,
That you'll be here and I'll be there,
Where once two fond hearts beat as one,
Two souls will wait in unison.

My love I'll leave; and nothing take,
Except your heart lest it might break,
Let not your salt tears fall on me,
Lest they disturb my dreams of thee.

Then leave me to my sombre sleep,
Where curlews call and willows weep,
In earth's brown bosom let me lie,
Grieve not: But think of me with joy.

Cruel death ferments the grapes of pain,
Where two were once; will one remain,
One kept a fatal rendezvous,
And the flickering flame of life withdrew.

Autumn Twilight

Bearded thistle-tops dance round my feet,
Along the headlands of the pastures as I pass,
And the zephyrs from the ocean soft and sweet,
Are dancing with the golden meadow grass.

How swiftly passes daylight overhead,
And languishes in evening's fond embrace,
And the sun that slumbers in its fiery bed,
Like a phoenix will reveal its morning face.

And the soulful sensuous sounds of evening song,
Have lured the weary reapers from the scene,
To tranquillity do the pastures now belong,
And every vague ephemeral thought recalls a dream.

Now darkness softly shuts the doors of day,
And draws the drapes across dream-drowsy eyes,
And I hear the distant echoes die away,
Of a curlew's cry in the solitude of skies.

From Helvick to Bunmahon's Copper Coast,
The reflection of the stars is billow tossed,
On nights like this remembrance is a ghost,
That talks to me of things I've loved and lost.

Lament For Summer

When dark December's glacial grip,
Claims a winter world it's own,
O'er the naked limbs of the trembling trees,
A grim grey cloak is thrown.
The grumbling gales from the freezing north,
Weaves a white, wind fashioned dream,
Of the whispering woods of summer,
Embracing, green on green.

And when the smoke swirls in the yard,
From a smouldering turf sod fire,
And sleet explodes on the windowpane,
And frost forms on the briar,
And round about the kitchen door,
The brawling birds complain,
And vie for death-delaying scraps,
In winter's dark domain.

And the gaunt blackthorns are dancing,
On a carpet of pure white,
And the earth beneath is brooding,
Through the stygian silent night,
And the thatch is weeping icy tears,
And the well is frozen o'er.
I crave with hopeless longing,
For the summer days of yore.

The Hawk

You stand motionless below the azure sky,
Among the realms where moist-lipped breezes blow,
And the compass of your golden gimlet eye,
Keeps watch on heaven above and the world below.

When veils of fog from the face of day depart,
A meandering mouse attracts your merciless glance,
And with folded wings you fall like a deadly dart,
On a random victim of cruel circumstance.

Remember Me

Tired from the tumult of the day,
I sought sanctuary in an evening glade,
And wandered from the well worn way,
To the whispering, tree sheltered shade.

The solace of silence, my soul beguiled.
The birds were songless on the bough.
As a mother's tale might soothe a child,
The furrows faded from my brow.

The ancient yews, like sentrys stood,
Resplendent in their garb of green,
Round forgotten grave-stones in the wood,
And the ravaged ruins, where a church had been.

The weathered words were ill-defined,
By wearing winters and weeping springs,
That I traced on tomb-stones, briar entwined,
My musing mind on mundane things.

Briar –bound beneath the tower bell,
One sagging stone, my attention drew,
From my foraging fingers, thorny tendrils fell,
And disclosed the secret the briars knew.

The words I read held me in thrall,
A lesson learnt and ne'er forgot.
Who penned those lines, I could not recall.
The poet's name, I still know not.

When heavens stars are all erased,
And night's dark arms, the world enfold,
A voice still speaks beyond the grave,
I cannot say, I was not told!

"Remember me as you pass by,
As you are now, so once was I,
As I am now, so you will be,
Prepare yourself to follow me."

The Legacy Of Love

I languish in the lingering light of evening,
When dusk's dark shadows silently unroll,
When peace pervades the gloaming –
And weary birds are homing,
And their whistling wings at sunset soothe my soul.

I am enchanted by the rustling leave's refrain,
When beneath the verdant sycamores I stroll,
Life is mingled joy and pain –
It croons again and yet again,
While twilight's mystic music soothes my soul.

When dew obscures the drowsy eyes of evening,
I recall love overflowed life's brimming bowl,
Though the winds of change are blowing-
And time; past us is tiptoeing,
The legacy of love still soothes my soul.

And even when the dawn is drenched with tears,
And the wan moon down the sky has ceased to roll,
Wearied by the wasted years –
And past feuds and future fears,
Still the colours of the sunrise soothe my soul.

Saint Declan's Well

By berried briar-brushed lanes I strolled along,
In sweet solitude "Toor's" autumn hills among,
Enraptured by cascading streams of song,
The feathered choirs poured on the evening air.

Untroubled, tranquil hours slipped away,
Until twilight drained the colours from the day,
And when on hillside and in glenside shadows lay,
A vague presence seemed to walk beside me there.

A lone cuckoo wing weary from the day,
To the setting sun sang one last roundelay,
Then with his melodies all stowed away,
In some shadowed sanctuary sought slumber there.

Exploding golden gorse had now grown quiet,
And the sun's last lurid lances of lingering light,
Could not repel the relentless march of night,
When a sacred well before me shimmered there.

Here Declan quenched his thirst in years of yore,
And the brimming well was blessed forever more,
Then his weary sandled steps turned towards Ardmore,
And still his presence haunts the evening air.

'Tis said sometimes when an evening's soft and still,
A phantom form strays across "Toor's" darkened hill,
And kneels beside the blessed well until,
Vague voices from Ardmore call him to prayer.

The Poet

His pen is inked to write of wrongs,
That torment man's existence,
And lay the blame where blame belongs,
With pervasive quiet persistence.

He sees God's face in the first primrose,
That struggles through the snow,
When memory's fountain overflows,
He sups from springs of long ago.

He's forged on the fires of despair,
Where the desolate are hurled,
His poems weep for the lost ones there,
With the tears of all the world.

He walks the rock-strewn paths of time,
To seek the hidden rose,
On every stone he carves a rhyme,
Where a blossom might repose.

He finds hope in battle's loud alarms,
Where a helping hand extends,
To the wounded wing in the leaden storms,
When foes reach out as friends.

Or perhaps he sings of mundane things,
Where rhyme and rhythm resonate,
Like the fluttering of folding wings,
Or a closing evening gate.

His words are host to passion's ghost,
When life's lamp is burning low,
He hears the last cry of the lost,
And the muffled step and slow.

When dusk is scented with the dew,
And brawling breezes bring the rain,
He wraps old tales in words anew,
And in love's old sweet refrain.

Evening

I am garlanded by evening's gentle hand,
The sea is stained by the last blush of the sun,
The shadows gather gold dust from the sand,
And with gratitude I bless the day that's done.

What worth would be the wealth of all the world,
If I could not linger here at evening's hour,
To see the little bud of yesterday unfurled,
And the dewy tears upon the fragrant flower?

My thoughts meander like a vagrant breeze,
Through the tranquil mystic mansions of my mind,
The lighted doors I open wide with ease,
The darkened doors I lock – and leave behind.

In the peaceful stillness silence reigns supreme,
Yet it seems to speak in whispered undertone,
"It is time to go to rest, and time to dream,
Tomorrow's songs are still to-day unknown".

Heaven In The Mist

The sun at dawn her gold dust scattered,
Down every path where I would play,
Those brief bright days that a child's heart treasured,
Still sing their songs of yesterday.

I loved the morning mist-moist meadows,
And I loved the twilight's brooding quiet,
And in the night dream-haunted shadows,
Played hide and seek with the starry light.

When encroaching dusk embraced and kissed,
The shadowed golden harvest sheaves,
There were hints of heaven in the mist,
And sacred songs in the evening breeze.

There by the frayed fringe of the ocean,
I sojourned at peace through the summer days,
Those who touched my heart; own my heart's devotion,
Their love stitched joy to my childish ways.

But I would weep when August died,
And the passive plough was rusted brown,
In the skirts of memory I would hide,
When I went back to the dismal town.

My Grandmother

Ballinacourty's waves are sighing,
In this soft May evening rain,
Here I wait as day is dying,
Though my waiting be in vain.

Spring promised sweet songs of summer,
Blossoms hid every hawthorn tree,
But the sands in life's short measure,
Were fast ebbing like the sea.

Sombre shadows were around you creeping,
Cruel fate would not be denied,
The angels were a vigil keeping,
Death waited at your side.

When May was in the meadows,
And flowers fringed the lane,
You passed through pains dark shadows,
To the peace of God's domain.

Though your songs are cloaked in silence,
And your footprints leave no trace,
In this peace I feel your presence,
And your fingers touch my face.

And the sea-mist paints your picture,
Where the plaintive curlews scream,
And to me you sometimes whisper,
In the vapours of a dream.

Still I watch the waves and wonder,
Across the tides of eighty years,
Could I tear time's veil asunder,
And see you through my tears.

The Glorious Game

Enchantment cloaks the Comeraghs when the dawn
is barely born,
And soft breezes stir the meadows of my mind,
And I hear the songbirds sprinkling their music on
the morn,
And a spool of mystic memories they unwind.

Fox and pheasant these hills have sheltered and
young rebels on the run,
When the fight for freedom set our land aflame,
With the rifle's ragged rattle and the garrulous
Thomson gun,
As the "Flying Columns" played war's deadly game.

And "Comeragh" wept with anguish when its
children's blood was spilt,
And Pat Keating died below its verdant side,
And in Coolnasmear's green pastures where his
brother Tom was killed,
Though we think of them with sorrow, we
remember them with pride.

But deadly days of darkness from that
glorious game ensued,
When a flawed and factious treaty was signed.
When brother fought with brother and
the sire disowned his brood,
And hope was scattered like rose petals on the wind.

But we have long restored the honour of
our once great Irish race,
And side by side we stand as comrades once again,
We'll no more beneath God's heaven
confront each other face to face,
But our foes face with the courage and
compassion of free men.

If I search among my mountains,
would I find it still the same,
When twilight lights its candles in the gloom?
But they are gone beyond my finding, the friends
who fell in freedom's name,
Still I seek them in the silence as the shadows
blanch and bloom.

The Tides Of Twilight

The tranquil tides of twilight talk to me,
From the reservoir of tales oft told before,
Still they weave their spells around me constantly,
As would whispering waves on some deserted shore.

When a winter world is drenched by driving rain,
And across confining banks, streams overflow,
Distended pregnant clouds tell me their pain,
As their waters shower down to make things grow.

Then springtime comes cavorting down the morn,
Like a seraph, whose wings once fettered are now free,
And she bears upon her breast, the newly born,
And with loving heart she offers it to me.

In the silence by the pausing, deeper stream,
I sit beneath the willow's sylvan shade,
And dream of all that was; or might have been,
In the lingering latticed light of a sheltered glade.

When no sound disturbs the stillness of the shade,
Throbs the heartbeat of the world beneath my feet,
The narcotic of it's sonorous serenade,
Lures me down dark leafy lanes; to dreams and sleep.

Song For Today

Can they ever hope to gain the prize?
Those who walk on wounded feet,
With heavy hearts and haunted eyes,
They drain the goblet of defeat.

And though their light so dimly glowed,
It touched not star or sun,
Still all along life's rocky road,
On bleeding feet they come.

Though the world rides roughshod over them,
And they're crushed beneath its heel,
May one brave heart their plight condemn,
And a better world reveal.

The Colligan River

Your symphonies surge through my mind,
Your face in dreams I see,
On your silver loom with sunlight thread,
You weave a web of songs for me.
I can hear your haunting melodies,
They throw a noose around my soul,
On the tranquil tides of memory,
I forget that I've grown old.

Daughter of some mountain stream,
You dance between flower blossomed banks,
And bird-song on the fragrant air,
To the river Gods give thanks.
As the sunbeams play upon your face,
They flash and flare like flowing gold,
And stars at night-time sojourn there,
To listen to your tales unfold.

You frolic down fog-frowning slopes,
And call farewell to Comeragh's Hill,
With forlorn hopes you try to turn,
The water wheel at Dower's Mill.
Then beneath the bridge you rush and race,
Where Ballyneety stems the tide,
And Rinn-na-Phooka's lonely face,
You kiss as towards the sea you glide.

By Shandon's sinuous sheltered shore,
On the flood you take your ease,
And the clash of ash from Fraher Field,
Is bourne on the breeze.
Then evening folds it's weary wings,
But for you no recompense of rest,
So take my dreams like fallen leaves,
That float upon your breast.

From Strandside's verdant wooded banks,
Lilts the language of the thrush,
He wraps his words in melody,
In twilight's haunted hush.
Then dusk descends dew-drenched and dim,
To pluck the day's remaining rose,
And the Colligan at journey's end,
In Dungarvan Harbour finds repose.

Black Dog

When melancholy's mantle has shrouded the mind,
We pray that the sun may rise,
To loosen the ligature of lethargy,
And brush bitter tears from our eyes.

When wild waves of woe crash onto the shore,
And depression's black dog ranges free,
Just one spark of hope may lighten the gloom,
And bring ease to our agony.

A calmness descends when the storm has gone,
And our fears for a while take flight,
Though despair's devil dog still lurks in his lair,
We forget how he howled in the night.

An impassive expression of passionless peace,
We present to the transient throng,
While the stigma of shame shades our tumbling tears,
We strive to garland our grief in song.

In a heart that is hurt it is ever the same,
When torment thrusts deep with the knife,
It's bloody, barbed blade has been whetted and honed,
On the grim grinding mill-stones of life.

Though we may endure the pangs and the pain,
Of the sharp crippling spears of despair,
The honey of hope still sweetens the cup,
Let us always remember 'tis there.

At The Gates Of Day

Down a misty morning path I walk alone,
While ancient rhymes go rambling through my mind,
And the chorus of the dawn in undertone,
Is strumming on the harpstrings of the wind.

I have walked these lonely laneways, man and boy,
In a timeless tranquil peace years can't erase,
Since long ago they heard my infant cry,
And their signature they've written on my face.

I'll gallivant to the golden gates of day,
While the saffron sun creeps over Helvick Head,
And the yellow whin with sensuous seductive sway,
Will lure late-rising bees from their honeyed bed.

In the dawn-streaked dome the skylark laughs aloud,
And spills fragments of his music on the morn,
His suspended silhouette clings to the cloud,
So flamboyant; yet somehow, so forlorn.

The wayward whispering waters of Dalligan's stream,
Slips sensuously into the tide's embrace,
Like a blushing bride who drifts in a vaporous dream,
As by her bride-groom's side she takes her place.

The familiar scenes that grace my every glance,
Impart a peace that nowhere else I'll know,
In the solitude of morn, I find romance,
And at evening; memories of long ago.

Sitting By The Fire

When night winds strummed on strings of rain,
And we sat content by the rose-red blaze,
From the fiddle you lured some old refrain,
As the flames absorbed your distant gaze.

So lovingly you touched the bow,
And coaxed to song with soft commands,
And sensuous stroking to and fro,
The fragile fiddle in you callused hands.

And the tunes curled round me like a vine,
In my mind they echoed all night long,
And threw a noose around the throat of time,
And re-echo still where dreams belong.

Then in sleepy soft serenity,
With the tenderness of the thistledown,
You'd touch my cheek and reluctantly,
Bid me goodnight 'ere I lay down.

When the lighthouse flung it's spears of flame,
Across the shoulders of the tide,
Death's cold hand crushed my heart with pain,
I've grown old and grey since the music died.

When recollections grapes I crush,
Their vintage wine is bittersweet,
As the evening song of a distant thrush,
And forgetfulness only sings in sleep.

And sometimes in the twilight's gloom,
The fiddle sings to me again,
It's notes re-echo round the room,
Where first I heard that old refrain.

The Fool

I sing my songs of harmony,
Of love and loss and things to be,
Of summer days and winter nights,
Of autumn's gold and spring's delights.

Of hearths of home and friendly fires,
Of secret smiles and heart's desires,
I sing of embers long grown cold,
And of friends I knew in days of old.

I sing of youth's swift passing years,
Of hopes and joys and brimming tears,
I sing of those who went astray,
And of broken hearts when dreams decay.

I sing of lamplight in the gloam,
And of sunsets when the boats come home,
I sing of peace and quiet content,
Of ecstasies and passions spent.

I sing my songs at the gates of day,
Dawn fills my soul with things to say,
I sing in tune with the singing birds,
Such songs a fool tries to sing with words.

Memories

Memories dance across the miles,
Of the years hardbeaten track,
Round every bend are tears and smiles,
As we go farther back.

And little zephyrs whisper things,
To lure us farther still,
To vaguer scenes on wilting wings,
Beyond the farthest hill.

'Tis there we hide the hurting heart,
And cruel words we can't revoke,
And the secrets stitched with devious art,
To the hem of memories cloak.

And here and there through smiles and tears,
Are dreams that turned to gold,
They light the laneways of the years,
That memory's spool unrolled.

Dream Of Me No More

Across the throbbing threshold of my heart,
In every thought I bore you tenderly,
When cupid's bow-string shot its sweetest dart,
Love overflowed its chalice just for thee.

Enveloped by enchantment's ecstasy,
To watch you waiting at the trysting place,
And the rose-blush on your cheek again to see,
As sighing you succumbed to my embrace.

You inspired sweet songs of love for me to sing,
Their melodies were meant to throng the years,
But to your loveliness I could no longer cling,
Now remember me with joy and unshed tears.

If I might perhaps at dusk invade your dreams,
When tremulous dreams of mine are long since 'oer,
And if grief perchance should shade these pleasant scenes,
Then love, I beg you! Dream of me no more.

Sanctuary

The little lamps of sunset are flickering in the stream;
And twilight tints the azure skies of June,
The green crown of the oak tree will soon with gold stars gleam,
And shed silver tears beneath the Harvest Moon.

As time went tiptoeing through the years,
it watched the world grow old,
From its lofty eyrie high upon the hill,
The sanctuary of its pensive peace did often me enfold,
In silence; when the days loud din grew still.

Often when I was weary, and had no strength left to fight,
And fearful I would falter in the fray,
It soothed my soul with solitude, at the dimming of the light,
In the rainbow tinted remnants of the day.

How many souls before me have sought its solace and its shade?
How many tears were shed beneath its boughs?
How many regrets were whispered? How many sighs relayed,
The loneliness of love's oft broken vows?

In this peaceful place at twilight, when I will be no more,
Some hurting heart as melancholy as mine;
Will find here in the silence, the strength it had before,
And the fortitude; life's highest hills to climb.

Just An Ordinary Day

The clock shouts in the darkness,
You scramble out of bed,
It seems hardly half and hour,
Since you lay down your head.

It would be lovely just to linger,
And ignore that traitor; time,
But the world would shudder to a halt,
If you're not at work by nine.

Speed and multi-tasking,
No resting on your oars,
Keep the pedal to the metal,
Do a day's work in two hours,

Noses to the grindstone,
Shoulders to the wheel,
No smoking and no joking,
No matter how you feel.

Don't swing the lead, no skiving off,
Always toe the line,
And keep your best foot forward,
Stop looking at the time.

Keep rushing and keep racing,
No glass ceilings in your way,
Keep you head down and look upward,
Every canine has his day.

"Going forward" is the buzz word,
You've no time for looking back,
But there's a thousand others trying,
To sneak up the inside track.

Time's Illusion

When eyes grow heavy with the weight of sleep,
And time is trundling to infinity,
So short this earthly vigil do we keep,
'Ere we forever find tranquility.

Unending days drift drowsily on and on,
And silent seasons slip by us unawares,
Until the illusion of eternal years is gone,
And every idle hour is a step upon life's stairs.

Then in the twilight of some transcendent day,
When sails are drifting homeward from the sea,
They will bear with solemn footsteps me away,
And illusion will be then reality.

When Evening Comes

When evening comes as evening must,
And stars across the heavens burn,
You and me that came from dust,
To dust again we will return.

The tides of time now rushing past,
Will sweep us one by one away,
Until on an alien shore we're cast,
At the twilight of some timeless day.

Though life is transient at best,
Let not despair destroy your days,
Let happiness be a welcome guest,
And drape every dawn with dream's bouquets.

Let the lamplighter of all the stars,
Reach out his hand to show the way,
Let him tear aside the prison bars,
Where heartache thrives, and dreams decay.

May your heart rejoice when springtime comes,
And summer sails on a sea of flowers,
When autumn's gold crowns the harvest homes,
And winter weeps in bare-boughed bowers.

When you've walked the distance of your days,
And the mile-stones one by one are passed,
God will guide you through life's darkening maze,
And forgive the failures of the past.

The Loner

I care not for the crowded road,
That onwards and upwards go.
I grow confused as the miles unfold,
In life's heaving ebb and flow.
But the hidden trail through the undergrowth,
Is where I know sweet content,
And in the silver note from the linnet's throat,
Where the blossomed bough is bent.

I hide away from the haunts of men,
In some friendly forest glade.
In the harmony of the leaves refrain,
And the flickering light and shade.
Where the electric flash of kingfisher blue,
Cuts across a crystal brook,
Some morning when May is drenched with dew,
And the hills have a hazy look.

Where the peaks are a panorama of purple,
And the mountains flare to flame,
With heather, whin, and whortle,
When summer comes again.
And borne on the breeze is a vixen's bark,
From a distant gloomy glen,
'Till the sound re-echoes in my heart,
Again and yet again.

And dreamy in the solitude,
I am Lord of untrodden leas,
Where only nature's songs intrude,
And my soul at last knows ease.
And when at dusk the sun descents,
Into the shadowed west,
And starlight reigns when twilight ends,
There undisturbed I'll rest.

Visions

In the rapture of the stillness when the weary
world grows quiet,
Vague visions fill the shadows and vague voices
fill the night,
Of the yesteryears that were stepping-stones to
better times ahead,
When a dream perchance sometimes came
true, when hope had all but fled.

Now silver streaks my thinning hair that once
flashed fires of gold,
When youth's laurel crown perched proudly
there, 'ere the spool of years unrolled,
The furrowed face and features, inked in by
time's cruel pen,
Recalls the harmony and hardship and the
heartbreak now and then.

Among the wreckage of the years shines the
shards of cherished dreams,
But the worthless weeds of wasted days lure
the lustre from their gleams,
All life is but a lottery that fate's whim might
well destroy,
May the hopes I harboured in my heart, fill
future days with joy.

In the footsteps of the fleeting days, the
years flew quietly by,
But the morn fulfilled it's promise, 'ere
evening stained the sky,
Now children play around my chair, with
love I watch them grow,
In their features mirrored I can see myself
long, long ago.

In my heart I'm hardly twenty, but the
mirror will not lie,
The years that sang their carefree songs
now scarcely heave a sigh,
Now other shoots are springing up, how
straight and strong they grow,
The roses that are blooming now were
planted long ago.

Graves's Well

When the light grows short on Helvick's Hill,
By Graves's crystal Well,
I wonder what mystic magical tales,
It's moss-mantled stones could tell.

Then a strange sad sense of stillness,
Lulls to sleep the evening flowers,
And the ghosts of lost beloved friends,
Lights other scenes and hours.

And a haunting hint of woodsmoke,
From the sighing sea-shore rolls,
Where the cheerful Caledonian girls,
Once smoked the herring shoals.

Then down the path by the fragrant pines,
With brimming pails they go,
Those girls I knew when the world was young,
Sixty yearning years ago.

And they pause in the pensive silence,
Beneath heaven's star-blossoming dome,
By the slumbering dream-haunted waters,
'Till the evening sails come home.

From the landlord's lodge on Helvick Head,
Two old ghosts meander down,
One is the Earl of Grandison,
And Lord Stuart from Villierstown.

They congregate in the moonlight,
With generations of a lost long ago,
Round the Well there's no servant or master,
And the stories of old ebb and flow.

They weave from the yarn of memories,
A tapestry of the tales they tell,
Of gun-runners; and shipwrecks; and smugglers,
As they lean on the arch of the Well.

Then the phantoms one by one leave me,
All alone with my thoughts and my tears,
With sighs of parting Graves's Well echoes,
As it's done for three hundred years.

Flights Of Fancy

If the dreams I have could somehow come true,
I would roam as the wind roams free,
I would throw a noose around a steed of stars,
And gallop far over a timeless sea.

I would sing my songs in a land of dreams,
Where never is worn the cloak of night,
On a silken sea 'neath the rainbow's arch,
I would sail forever with wild delight.

I would amble along the Appian Way,
With the slaves and soldiers of ancient Rome,
I'd see the Bridge of Sighs and the Coliseum,
Where Christians of old to the lions were thrown.

I would travel back to Greece and Troy,
And meet those men of the warrior bone,
And stare in awe as the Sphinx was carved,
From a blemished buttress of desert stone.

I'd seduce fair Helen with rustic charms,
And I would kiss fair Helen on the lips,
Then I'd flee forever from her fatal arms,
And the face that launched a thousand ships.

I'd see the Hanging Gardens of Babylon,
The Spice Road I would walk with the Bedouin,
I would dance in the dawn around the Pyramids,
To her palace Cleopatra would invite me in.

Yes, away to the ends of the earth I'd go,
To where the Isles of the Orient flame,
And when the crystal sun sets beyond the Nile,
Aphrodite would call my name.

Pictures Of The Past

Come in old friend and rest awhile,
Sit by the fire with me,
We'll pluck the rose of yesteryear,
From the briar of memory.

As the fire paints pictures of the past,
With the brush-strokes of the blaze,
From the gloom will recollection reach,
To turn times tattered page.

We'll peruse a portrait in the flames,
That will summon up a dream,
And bridge the gulf to youthful years,
Where pain was unforeseen.

We'll wander down dark leafy lanes,
Where lilts a laughing voice of old,
That tinted days with rainbow hues,
And thatched the stars with gold.

And eyes that paled God's azure arch,
But shone alas too brief and bright,
Now death has built a hermitage,
In two old hearts tonight.

As two old dreamers by the fire,
Watch while the years unfold,
The tangled threads of memory,
They forget that they are old.

Morning And Music

I've been blessed by the birth of a beautiful child,
A miraculous, marvellous being,
To be her champion and slave is my heart reconciled,
And her guardian in grey days and green.

A vagrant salt tear from love's fountain o'er spills,
At the gift of a small sleepy smile,
As contented she drifts to dreams far away hills,
To cavort with the angels awhile.

She has winnowed the grain from the chaff of the years,
By her side I will stand and belong,
Her faint whimpers at night from vague baby fears,
Stirs the star-softened silence to song.

My heart is a bird in her baby-soft hand,
From it's grasp I will never fly free,
On love's rising tide she will soon understand,
She is morning and music to me.

The Clown

I laughed at the clown in the circus ring,
As he danced with a dog at the end of a string,
Then he told us the dog could count and sing,
And knew the alphabet.

I laughed and laughed 'till my sides were sore,
As the dog spelt words I never heard before,
And proclaimed with a howl one and one was four,
I laughed 'till my cheeks were wet.

To be a clown, I thought, on a daisied floor,
And to hear folks call "Encore! Encore!",
And to make them happier than they were before,
Was as good as life could get.

With a bow he bounced from the fun-filled tent,
But I saw him again as I homeward went,
And the white-washed face made for merriment,
Seemed to echo with laughter yet.

Then I saw his eyes and have yet to see,
Two deeper pools of melancholy,
With one brief glance he revealed to me,
A sadness that I can't forget.

Then I realised in the book of life,
Between the covers lurk pain and strife,
And neither clown or king can evade grief's knife,
Nor the requiems of regret.

Spectators

In the maudlin mists of musing, I see the rock-strewn road of life,
That the threads of time have stitched to memory's cloak.
When I'm too weary to be wakeful, and not tired enough for sleep,
In the eloquence of silence appear pictures in the smoke.

They come and go like phantoms as they dance above the fire,
And voices half-forgotten fill my mind,
The good times and the bad times; the things I did or didn't do,
Are swept up and swirl around me, like dead leaves in autumn wind.

Happy hands were raised in welcome;
and hands brushed away the tears,
When I came and when I left them in their grief,
But the ribbon road before me, ever lured me and cajoled me,
And the things I thought eternal, at the bitter end were brief.

I know it's futile to be fretting at what I did or should have done,
Fate won't be frustrated or denied,
Whether days deny their promise or good fortune smiles upon us,
We were merely dumb spectators in the space we occupied.

The Blessing Of The Boats

When May fanned the flames of the summer,
And the sun's scarlet lips kissed the sea,
From the riggings rippled remnants of rainbows,
Of the boats rafted up to the Quay.

A mad pageant of cascading colours,
Greeted the gay crowds on the shore,
And the sound of a harpsichord playing,
Wafted out through a half-open door.

Then the Priest raised his hand in a blessing,
And each heart an "amen" did intone,
And implored Him, who once walked on the water,
To bring all the lost seafarers home.

We cast off our lines and reached past the Cunnigar,
With Abbeyside's ancient church on the lee,
From "the Lookout" the seagulls were silently staring,
And our sails sang the songs of the sea.

Against our bows the billows were breaking,
As the prayer left our trembling lips,
Have pity, O Lord! On Thy children,
Who go down to the sea in ships.

Then we saw on the distant horizon,
Where ocean and heaven were one,
A phantom flotilla of tall ships,
Lit by the last rays of the sun.

Their sails hung in shreds from the yardarms,
As out there at worlds-end they converged,

And their hulls shone with streamers of seaweed,
And the seas round their rotten ribs surged.

In the distance they were watching and waiting,
Until the "Wreaths of Remembrance" fell,
On the turbulent waves of the ebb-tide,
Then the ghost ships seemed to signal farewell.

When a breeze stirred the shape of the shadows,
We could see the gaunt ghost ships no more,
They had vanished like the mist of the morning,
In their quest for a lost sunset shore.

'Tis said! Forever they search endless oceans,
For safe harbour by some sheltered strand,
On a shore far beyond where the sun sets,
But their footprints will no more stain the sand.

Time has enshrined them in legend,
Men who sailed towards ten thousand suns,
And who died in the terrors of the tempest,
That thundered like ten thousand guns.

Then our flag-festooned convoy turned homewards,
And we each felt in some strange way alone,
As we tied-up in the silence of sadness,
Each nursed a small grief of our own.

And the soft silken threads of our memory,
Will forever to our hearts tightly bind,
The shadow shrouded ships in the sunset,
That sail over the seas of our mind.

Let Me Dream

I hear again old haunting melodies,
In the incessant sibilant sighing of the sea,
When the evening light is tangled in the trees,
'Tis then it sings it's sweetest songs to me.

But I cannot understand the wistful words,
That are whispering among mist moistened air,
They're the secret of the little singing birds,
That wind; and wing; and wave; forever share.

And the rainbow does not now to me reveal,
The glory of it's colours bright and bold,
And it's silvered charms the moon from me conceal,
And the setting sun now hoards it's gleaming gold.

As radiant as the rose in summer blooms,
In winter it will wither and decay,
It's narcotic fragrance now no heart illumines,
It's lustre with the summer fades away.

Where once the wavelets sparkled in the bay,
Their silver sheen has dried to dusty gold,
And time's ebbing tide stole all my songs away,
Now evening comes, and I am growing old.

Yet, do not quench awhile the flickering fire,
But let me lay where broken billows gleam,
And listen to last songs of hearts desire,
And for awhile in nearly darkness let me dream.

Stolen Beauty

We gather the fragrant spring flowers,
From the fields where their colours belong,
And confine in a cage the song-bird,
And imprison his beautiful song.

Do we care that the bloom of the petals,
Will wither and die and decay?
And never sounded the bird-song so lovely,
As in the bosom of blossom-boughed May.

Do we care we have silenced the music,
And dimmed the lights on the dawn's carousel,
And stolen spring's beauty from others,
As long as all with our own world was well?

When we selfishly forage life's favours,
Do we care if we trample upon,
Those who share God's gifts with each other,
And still believe that we do them no wrong?

Are we guests or captives, I wonder!
In our gardens of avarice and greed?
Did the seedling of life that was planted,
In us; grow, not a flower- but a weed?

The Fields Of The Starry Flowers

*Dedicated to the unbaptised children who were denied burial in
consecrated ground, and who were often buried in secret under cover of
darkness in disused graveyards like Kilrush.*

In coffins made of rough-hewn slabs,
adorned with lime-wash white,
With the muffled steps of sack-wrapped
feet they carried us into the night.
And the fields of the starry flowers were blossoming overhead,
On our first and final journey to sleep among the dead.

Branded and betrayed as outcasts, unsanctified and unclean,
By crozier bearing princes robed in crimson and carmine,
In consecrated ground forbidden to sleep beneath its sward,
When no water of Baptism on our dying heads was poured.

Whey were we so rejected? What was the terrible deed,
That separated us from the Saviour in our hour of greatest need?
Our only crime was dying when we could not stay alive,
And the fever and the hunger ensured we would not survive.

A burning sack upon a stick lit our pathway through the gloom,
When they laid us here in secret where a field-stone marked our tomb.
Denied a blessing's comfort, but we will forever stay,
Close to him born in a stable, who never turned a child away.

They laid us here 'ere life began, in Kilrush's grave-gouged field,
Beside the ruined chapel where the weeping neighbours kneeled.
Their clandestine task accomplished, they slipped away into the night,
Guided down the briar-brushed laneway by a torch's flickering light.

Here we lie with our friends around us in this City of the Dead,
Forgotten by those who loved us, their tears are too long shed.
But God's memory is eternal, through times turbulent ebb and flow,
As the years have crowded past us, we have waited here below.

But the scales of justice will balance when the last long day is done,
And God's arm will reach around us, and he will say "my children, come!"
Condemned no more to darkness, contentment will at last be ours,
As we walk with the Lord forever, through the fields of starry flowers.

Secret Silent Tears

He who stands by the bitter grave,
All alone, aloof and cold,
Is 'oft by a vagrant tear betrayed,
That down a pale cheek rolled.
That scalding, salted drop revealed,
Grief's tormented atmospheres,
Where went the one whose legacy,
Was secret silent tears.

Softly whispered words of sympathy,
Are hanging in the air.
To drift away on a vagrant breeze,
Though he hardly seems aware.
But if we could lift the cloak of grief,
That will shroud the empty years,
We would find an overflowing Well,
Of secret silent tears.

Grievous loss inflicts a wound,
That in our hearts remain,
And the tumult of time's turning wheel,
Piles the passing years with pain.
And dreams that danced in the dawns of love,
Are now faint with faceless fears,
And in the shadows no one sees,
The secret silent tears.

There are those who beat an anguished breast,
And on sorrow's shoulders lean,
And cruel grief and desolation,
Is on their faces plainly seen.
But subdued distress is as eloquent,
If colder it appears,
And eyes that dwell in death's domain,
Shed secret silent tears.

The Village Of Abbeyside

As I saunter down the village streets at evening,
The sky is thatched with roses in the west,
At Organ's Pier the little boats are sleeping,
And twilight tempts a weary world to rest.

In silhouette the church is quietly brooding,
Watching for the monks of old on Friar's Walk,
Are their murmured prayers on the silence still intruding?
And do their ghosts glide past, wan faces white as chalk?

In pensive peace round the old churchyard I wander,
And peruse moss-mantled names on ancient stone,
Some beyond reflection's reach make me pause and ponder,
Among memorials familiar as my own.

And from the twilit porticoes of dreaming,
Scenes long-forgotten dance in the dimming light,
Their jewelled gowns with memories are gleaming,
Down time's long lane; we waltz; with lost delight.

In my mind I see a castle in the sunset,
Where McGraths of by-gone ages once held sway,
Now no pageantry or pennants grace it's turret,
All are crushed beneath the burden of decay.

At the "Poor Man's Seat" I hear vague voices telling,
Of old sailing ships and shipmates from the past,
The ghosts of lost seafarers are reminiscing,
Of shipwrecks, shattered spars, and broken masts.

The same salt-water yarns fill every evening,
Until reflections seem to ripple on the tide,
Of Dungarvan boats for foreign harbours leaving,
Sailing slowly past the Pond at Abbeyside.

My memory-haunted soul overflows with sadness,
As night's curtains on my village softly fall,
From King Street, John-Joe Young strolls through the darkness,
To stop awhile and stare; by the harbour wall.

Now Strandside is quietly dreaming in the gloaming,
As Shear's Street and Slate Lane I leave behind,
To pursue the peaceful pageant of my roaming,
Abbeyside! You haunt the mansions of my mind.

Blooms Of Distant Dreams

Tonight I walk at midnight's hour, solitude to find,
Along the streets of loneliness to soothe a seething mind,
No footsteps steal the stillness, save the echo of my own,
As the night wind sings it's dirges in a sombre undertone.

The pavements leap with lashing rain that I neither note nor feel,
I'm cursed by despair's dark growling dog that on my shoulders kneel,
He crouches there with glaring eyes and ferocious fearsome mien,
And tears to shreds the peace of mind, that lately mine had been.

The tyranny of transient time that sanctions peace and pain,
Wields an iron fist in a velvet glove and will ever do the same.
Despair is a cold companion around the ashes of the years,
As the rain-washed streets of loneliness hide the torrents of my tears.

I feel the weight of all the world upon my shoulders lie,
No one can understand my pain; they scorn me when I cry,
The prison bars no one can see, nor the dungeons in my mind,
Nor decaying blooms of distant dreams by despairs dark chains
confined.

Caille Beara An Tsean Phobail

Did you pander to some pagan God of old,
When you spilled your sweat to elevate these stones,
And build this tomb of massive monoliths,
To shelter your dead chieftain's bleaching bones?

Was it love that stirred your heart to labour here,
Or uncompromising ancient archaic laws?
Were you a peasant, or perhaps a serf or slave,
Downtrodden; forever clutching at life's straws?

How many times with daybreak in your eyes,
Did you walk through meadows whispering in the rain?
And how many sultry sunsets saw you plod,
Worn and weary homeward; bent with pain?

Did your chieftain dream he'd always be revered,
While above his breast the silent stones still stand,
Or know his name was only written on the wind,
And his pedigree on a page of shifting sand?

Five thousand years have their well-worn pathways trod,
Where "Sean Phobal's" fog softened storm moans,
The passer-by asks not "who slumbers here?"
But " who's ancient hands once raised these monstrous stones?"

When at last the scales are balanced at the end,
For king, or chieftain, warrior, serf or slave,
In times torn book all names are writ the same,
And everyone is equal in the grave.

Shadow Seekers

The wisps of straw were scattered round,
The woven twigs; the plaited grass,
The broken nest defiled the ground,
And the shattered speckled eggs alas.

A blackbird weeps upon the bough,
And flings her sorrow on the morn,
Her once sweet songs are silent now,
Her heart is pierced by grief's cruel thorn.

As to his vomit a dog returns,
They feast upon the fruits of fear,
The brutes in whom belligerence burns,
And who answer kindness with a sneer.

Now folks are fearful in their homes,
They dread the sound of breaking glass,
The torture and the broken bones,
And the torment that will never pass.

Frail folk for whom times sands have run,
Lie battered; bleeding on the ground,
Their festering fear can't be undone,
They are terror-stricken at every sound.

Like gloating gluttons they gorge on crime,
The shadow-seeking faceless few,
Yet we hear "Forgive Them!"every time,
"For they know not what they do"

The Stranger

Will some stranger turn the faded page,
Perhaps when the world's asleep,
With the melancholy mien of a hurting heart,
Grains of comfort there to reap?

And will perhaps some verse of mine,
Some simple sounding rhyme,
Reveal a rose among the thorns,
Across the sands of time?

Words that were planted in my soul,
And watered with my tears,
And love and laughter made them bloom,
In myriad atmospheres.

And may the night speed swiftly by,
And may that heart find peace,
When dawn has dimmed the silver stars,
May the silent suffering cease.

And I won't know the stranger's pain,
And I won't know his grief,
But I might sense in some strange way,
That my song brought a soul relief.

For Whom The Bell Tolls

My love! Are you planting roses?
Beneath this sullen sky,
Your eyes are bright with teardrops,
And your lips make no reply.

And why so sad and sombre?
Are you troubled at your task?
And are you digging far too deep,
For roses? May I ask.

Surely, this is no day for roses!
When winter's wild winds weep,
All roses love the springtime,
And still your solemn silence keep.

You! Who have been my lifelong love,
Through seasons fraught and fair,
Now heap the silence 'round me,
As if I wasn't there.

You pledged that you would love me,
Forever and a day,
Though content I'd lie in your embrace,
You turn your face away.

Please forgive my foolish questions,
It's a grave you make I see,
Stones lean like drunken sentinels,
'Round this resting place to be.

And the roses multi-coloured,
I see scattered on the ground,
'Ere this dismal day is ended,
Will wither on the mound.

Far away a bell is tolling,
Showering sadness 'oer the lea,
Who will answer it's soulful summons?
Dear God! It tolls for me.

The Alchemy Of Love

Within a graveyard's grim recess,
Wistful; I watched a woman pray,
Her shopping basket close did keep,
A moment snatched from the drudge of day.

By a moss-upholstered stone she knelt,
And softly spoke as if she knew,
There, listened one attentively,
Where rampant waving grasses grow.

She talked of all the mundane things,
That filled her fleeting days with care,
As evening drowsed with flower-full hands,
Where a lost love lay and listened there.

Then I discerned a tiny smile,
As thought love had lured the dark away,
The fires that once had burned so bright,
Still warmed the woman and the clay.

The close communion which endures,
Beyond the boundaries of the grave,
Is the promise and the mystery,
That makes the broken-hearted brave.

Then she sighed "Adieu!" and waved farewell,
Her basket held close by her side,
And said, "tomorrow, I'll come by again!"
In love's alchemy, he had not died.

Summer In Ballinclamper

I dream of the little potato fields;
Where in summer I would lie,
Among the crimson poppies,
Beneath a blue lark-lilting sky.

Then the thrush and finch and linnet,
Sprinkled songs upon the day,
And from the pasture-patterned hillside,
Rang the cuckoo's roundelay.

Then all the world was singing;
Summer's sweetest symphony,
And from distant foam-fringed caverns,
Boomed the bass drums of the sea.

Then the blackbird's playful piping,
Floated faintly down the wind,
And reverberates forever,
In the meadows of my mind.

The Turning Tide

In the vague voice of the western wind,
Memory's whispers waft to me,
From across the turbulent ocean,
To the shores of a silent sea,
I'm a transient bird of passage,
For whom fate will soon decide,
When it's time to slip life's moorings,
At the turning of the tide.

Then I'll step aboard my sea-scarred boat,
Thought it's ancient planks are rotten,
It has stood me well in wind and wave,
On voyages half forgotten,
I'll navigate towards the setting sun,
And trim the sails alone,
Though my hand will hold the tiller,
God's hand will guide me home.

And reveries of long ago,
Are with rose fragrance scented,
I'll stand on deck in the dusk of day,
My soul by dreams enchanted,
As memory's fingers turn the page,
Other sights and scenes awaken,
I'll sail across a silent sea,
By sweet sadness overtaken.

For life is such a fragile friend,
In times remorseless pageant,
The seductive splendour of it's charms,
Is on fate's weird whim dependent,
When the curfew bell at last is tolled,
And I am by years surrounded,
May I sail home on sleeping seas,
By waves of woe unwounded.

A King Without A Crown

The fields grow dim where I have toiled and tilled,
In the pleasing peace beneath the darkening dome,
My fountains of content are overfilled,
By the coins that in life's wishing well were thrown.

'Tis wondrous to be a king without a crown,
If your kingdom though a few scant acres be,
My subjects I survey as dusk drifts down,
When I pass they bow their blossomed heads to me.

And my subjects are the song-birds in the trees,
They call me from my couch to greet the day,
When they wake me with their morning melodies,
I bless them as I did when down I lay.

And wild flowers in the paddocks by the sea,
Incline their painted faces as I pass,
And dance their sensuous breeze-stirred dance for me,
And the timid ones that hide in the heaving grass.

When evening's burning embers stain the sun,
With purple-splendoured shades at day's demise,
Eyes wet with dew, will weeping darkness come,
As a fleet of starry ships sail down the skies.

In my small kingdom I have toiled and tilled,
And beneath God's guidance I have reaped and sown,
The harvest home with happiness is filled,
And the monarch rests contented on his throne.

Death In The Afternoon

The Matador in his arrogance stood arched like a bow,
And inhaled the sweet scent of success.
His razor sharp rapier poised aloft for the blow,
That would end the bull's dreadful distress.

He pirouetted aside from every rage-blinded rush,
Of the bewildered and pain-maddened beast.
The rapier flashed once in the breath-holding hush,
And the strongest succumbed to the least.

The Matador turned and bowed low to the crowd,
To acknowledge each blood-soaked accolade.
As the plaudits showered 'round him he stood peacock proud,
And strutted 'round in a victory parade.

But the rapier had missed that one vital part,
Where the fires of life faintly flamed,
And courage consumed that still beating heart,
The bull arose though blood-blinded and maimed.

Arrogance and ignorance, self-importance and scorn,
From reality sets fools far apart.
'Twas a lesson unlearned when a rapier-sharp horn,
Tore straight through the Matador's heart.

The bull sank to his knees with soft blood-misted sighs,
As the red dust in torment he ploughed,
Then the dark drapes of death drew their shades down his eyes,
His head dropped; and he bowed to the crowd.

Reflection

My heart rejoiced when the morning rose,
Bloomed in the scented dawns of June,
But I never thought time would impose,
It's shadows on life's afternoon.

I watched the world with wondrous eyes,
And thought my dreams would all come true,
As I climbed the hills of paradise,
Time's darkening clouds obscured my view.

Too brief a glimpse – too short a stay,
To savour the sweetness of the rose,
Then time's dark hand on my white hair lay,
Life's drapes to draw – life's book to close.

House Of Dreams

In my heart I've built a house for you,
With walls of stone and roof of thatch,
It's little windows vague with dew,
It's half-door leaning on the latch.

There are rambling roses everywhere,
And whitewash gleams on the garden wall,
The flickering flame of a driftwood fire,
Makes the shimmering shadows leap and fall.

And when we turn the evening key,
And leave the world to the realms of night,
Two hearts will beat in harmony,
Love's lamp will be our guiding light.

Within this quaint and crooked house,
Our dreams will bloom and blossom there,
In love's embrace on an ancient couch,
Our hearts; our souls; our love; we'll share.

And when the tide torments the shore,
And the storm shouts at the sullen sky,
When wailing winds weep at the door,
We'll be soothed to sleep by it's lullaby.

The Far-Off Fields Of Home

When a blackbird on an evening bough is singing,
It lures me back again to childhood hours,
Where poppies built a bonfire in the furrows,
To warm the hearts of potato blossom flowers.

I see heaving golden-hearted purple blossoms,
Undulating like a scented surging sea,
And those far-off fertile fields of Ballinacourty,
In evening's quiet, still bloom again in me.

Where an old man walked behind an aged pony,
That sure-footed through the flowers pulled the plough,
In my young heart that old man walked on water,
Long ago he owned my heart; and he owns it now.

In his gentle way my childhood fears he soothed,
When he made a fiddle sob at dim of day,
I have followed his fragile footsteps broken-hearted,
Since he left me here alone; and went away.

Shawled by passing time, and the year's long shadows,
In the shrouded dusk where life's withered leaves have blown,
I recall the flowery fields and verdant meadows,
Where an old man and a child reaped what they'd sown.

In those fields of fondness I am now a stranger,
The old friends I once knew are now all gone,
Kindly neighbours with whom I used to linger,
Under Ballinroad's green sward at peace sojourn.

Spears of light still shine from the lighthouse lantern,
Across the turbulent tides of Dungarvan Bay,
And the whispering waves across the sands are creeping,
To wrap their sensuous arms around Clonea.

Heavy hangs the silence now at sunset,
And in my heart the purple blossoms blow,
Where and old man walks behind an aged pony,
And still calls me from the mists of long ago.

This Too Will Pass Away

In the sensuous solace of silence,
When passion weaves it's wondrous delight,
And you sip the sweet nectar of ardour,
And love floods the dark spaces of night.
And youth's blossoms still bloom on your features,
And dawn's rose it's coral colours display,
On the blue-tinted canvas of morning,
But this will, in time, pass away.

When the tendrils of gloom twine around you,
And every dream has withered and waned,
And the wine in grief's goblet is bitter,
And love's rose with rejection is stained.
And the millwheels of hope have stopped turning,
Buried deep in despair's foetid clay,
And you dread every dawn and each dawning,
But, this too, will in time pass away.

Regrets

I regret some things that I have done,
Through years that have come and years that have gone,
The hurtful words I will always rue,
The mistakes I made that I can't undo.

But the great regret that I can't resolve,
Is not just the wrongs I am guilty of,
But the times I turned my face from view,
Make me regret far more things I didn't do.

The Fires Of Spring

The fires of spring will one day die,
And ignite again no more,
Like the echoes of a last goodbye,
On some deserted shore,
And time's unpausing pendulum,
Will steal the hours away,
Too soon; too soon; will the morning sun,
Be the dawn of yesterday.

Autumn's breath will revive no more,
The languid golden leaves,
That are drifting down the evening air,
On the wings of a whispering breeze.
Though we wish lost moments to repeat,
Where throbs a human heart,
The hours creep by on velvet feet,
And summer days depart.

Then let us greet each golden morn,
As if each one was our last.
Time's mill wheel grinds youth's golden corn,
While flows life's waters past.
Your harvest reap while sunlight shines,
Upon dream's distant hill,
And do not wait till evening's chimes,
Obscures the idle mill.

Think not then of darker days,
But sip the wines of spring,
Nor languish in life's rutted ways,
While yet there's time to sing.
And all things young are growing old,
And all things old must die,
And the fires of spring grow grey and cold,
As soon must you and I.

The Dancers

When night recites it's rhymes of rain,
And the tide is tearing up the shore,
With wailing words the winds complain, ·
As they prowl outside the kitchen door.

While I sit in pensive solitude,
The memories of the past hold sway,
On my musing a fiddle's notes intrude,
From long ago and far away.

The music trembles in the gloom,
I hear it's sobbing, keening call,
Faint laughing voices fill the room,
Of friends now gone beyond recall.

Now shadows shimmer on the wall,
And ghosts dance in the lamplight's glow,
Their forms unseen; and unheard footfall,
Sway in time with the tunes of long ago.

I hear a voice soar clear as light,
Faint and far and out of reach,
As the singer follows the fiddles flight,
Though he sings beyond the gates of speech.

We were young but the world grew old,
And the velvet-footed years crept past,
As the tapestry of time unrolled,
Now 'tis sixty springs since I saw them last.

On a night like this when the fire burns low,
Heaven may open it's gates perchance,
For fond friends to gather again below,
And take the floor for one final dance.

An Evening In May

The bud-bursting leaves of the summer-soft foliage
Flutters and flickers in the white lanes of May,
And seduces with the sway of their sensuous dancing,
Waltzing rainbow-hued butterflies, from fields far away.

And sickle-like briars stretch thorny hands out to hold you,
From the grass crowded margins of the light-latticed lane,
And bluebells are blowing, where the stream's slowly flowing,
And falls apple-blossom like a shower of pink rain.

Wing weary warblers are frantically foraging,
For a ravenous raucous insatiable brood;
But somehow finds the time for a sweet tree-top chorus,
That pours peace on the heart, and lights every dark mood.

Grey clouds in the gloaming bind their vaporous tresses,
With remnants of ribbon left by sunset's last ray,
From the hems of the evening hang the tassels of twilight,
And darkness descending dims the eyes of the day.

Two Loves

In my summer-robed rose garden,
Among the gossamer clinging dew,
With the scents of summer laden,
Captivates my soul anew.

And the myriad tinted roses,
Turn their faces to the sun,
Like a rainbow that reposes,
When the summer showers are gone.

I'm enchanted by their beauty,
I am drunk on fragrant air,
And their gold and crimson bounty,
To standing stops me there.

They are opium to my senses,
But my heart is stirred anew,
By a golden headed princess,
That I am in love with too.

There's a quiet secluded corner,
Beyond the garden of the rose,
In a sheltered shady arbour,
That my other true love knows.

When the evening shades to shadow,
And the twilight brings repose,
In my heart they'll bloom together,
The primrose and the rose.

Unkind Words

My mind revolves 'round redundant rhymes,
My heart throbs with a troubled beat,
My thoughts are thronged with olden times,
Regrets are strewn around my feet.

The cherished dream so swiftly flown,
Since autumn filled the fields with flame,
The heart in harmony with my own,
Throbs in ecstasy to another's name.

I'm tormented by cruel things I said,
That tolled for dreams, a requiem,
Like hawks they hover round my head,
They've torn love's blossom from the stem.

Now summer sings it's old, old themes,
And winter flings it's spears of pain,
Regret replaces springtime's dreams,
And unkind words I can't reclaim.

The Old Man And The Child

We leaned across an evening gate,
In the languid long ago,
When the world was quiet in the evening light,
And the tides of time ebbed slow.

Sounds from the fields were hushed and still,
In the silence softened gloam,
When the lamp of day was stowed away,
And the cows meandered home.

Sixty springs have filled the fields,
Since last I lingered there,
Where daylight waits at evening's gates,
To hide in night's dark hair.

Content was captured in a sigh,
As twilight's wheel was turned,
And shadow's broom swept from the gloom,
The suns last rays that burned.

And peace stepped down the stairs of day,
As though to meet a lover,
And a molten moon illumed the gloom,
And stitched silver stars to the clover.

And still we stood and still we stared,
'Till the azure hours had fled,
And love's flag unfurled in that perfect world,
"We'll go home!" was all he said.

The Old Home

The walls are stained by years and rain,
In the yard the weeds are waving,
Round the threshold stone winds mew and moan,
In the lingering light of evening.

Cobwebs stream from the sagging beams,
That support the blackened thatching,
And whitewash falls from the crumbling walls,
And the door leans on the latching.

Spectral shadows crawl across the hall,
On silent feet advancing,
And dead brown leaves stirred by the breeze,
On the kitchen floor are dancing.

There's an eerie quiet in the dying light,
And the air is soft with sadness,
And the hills around are bereft of sound,
Where rang children's shouts of gladness.

To the realms of song did my soul belong,
But far from me now they're keeping,
The dew's damp breath drips grief and regret,
Like me; the "Old Home" is weeping.

With protesting cries to the sombre skies,
Creak hinges red and rusting,
As I close the gate briars bid me wait,
With their thorny hands a'clutching.

The mind of man since time began,
Seeks solace at longs day's ending,
And turns towards home in the gathering gloam,
When life with death is blending.

The Vision And The Dream

We were slaves and serfs down the ages,
From our shackles we at last struggled free,
But self-serving greed-driven new masters,
Restrained us with far more subtly.

Captivated and enthralled by their eloquence,
As they unveiled their ridiculous schemes,
Those monuments to arrogance and ignorance,
That destroyed our hopes and our dreams.

They were the new gods of creation,
Ensconced on their ivory thrones,
On the fat of our nation they feasted,
While mere mortals sucked scraps from the bones.

We are chained to their unjust conventions,
And by their shackles of shame we are bound,
And their selfish aspirations and intentions,
Without mercy grind us into the ground.

We're condemned to a servitude of silence,
And manacled to the monstrous greed,
Of the bankers and the builders of cities,
For whom avarice is a god and a creed.

Let us lend no ear to their whining,
Let us cast off the chains one more time,
For the thief in the pristine white collar,
Let his punishment equal his crime.

Let the hammer strike sparks from the anvil,
Let us once more for battle prepare,
Let the supercilious smirks on their faces,
Freeze in fear as our swords cleave the air.

Let our anger be a tumultuous torrent,
Let passion and pain prime our pride,
Let our beacon be the dream and the vision,
Of our patriot leaders who died.

A Perfect Peace

Dawn stole the silver from the stars,
And the dew-drenched sun turned the morn to gold,
It brought back summers of long ago,
'Ere the heaped-up years had made me old.

A sun-browned boy played on the beach,
As if the day could not be too long,
His delighted cries recalled for me,
How fast the years have bloomed and gone.

I saw him listen to a shell,
I saw him skim the flattened stone,
I saw him sail his little boat,
In the rock-pools where he reigned alone.

I drowsed and dreamed on the wave-worn shore,
His childish joy a sweet undertone,
To the lullaby of the singing sea,
In a world of wonder, once my own.

The serenity of the whispering waves,
The breath of the breeze from the soft south-east,
The happiness of one small boy,
Infolded me in a perfect peace.

Dungarvan

Dungarvan of the sailing ships of yore,
Nestling between the Comeraghs and the sea,
I will forever leave my footprints on your shore,
Where The Cunnigar's foaming flood-tide croons to me.

When evening's mantle clothes the Comeragh's peaks,
Where little rivers rush to distant seas,
I feel the throbbing of your heart beneath my feet,
And hear the sweetness of your songs in every breeze.

Your haunting lullabies lull me to sleep,
And you dance among my dreams when night winds blow,
Fond images of you I forever keep,
Since first I saw your face long, long ago.

On The Lookout wall I lean when day declines,
And shadows scowl on Cruchaun's slumbering slopes,
The ancient church at Abbeyside the dusk defines,
And the little boats tug at their mooring ropes.

When peace profound clings to the skirts of day,
And I stand upon the threshold stone alone,
I am lured by memory's melodies away,
And old Dungarvan sings to me in undertone.

On the trembling tides of thought that come and go,
Beyond confining casements of the will,
I see the Viking ships in Shandon's ebb and flow,
And Deise chiefs still dwell on Gallows Hill.

If I Had Never ...

If I had never listened to the Linnet's song,
And the tuneful troubadours of the feathered throng,
If I had never heard streams gossip as they go,
Barren would my existence be: I know.

If I had never watched the passing years parade,
I would not have known shine follows after shade,
I would not have seen day's sunrise and demise,
Or known for everyone who laughs – there's one who cries.

If I had never learned 'twas wrong to pray,
To man-made Gods that stand on feet of clay,
I never would have known when nought remains,
That heaven makes amends for all life's pains.

If I had never seen love's light in another's eyes,
Through a darkened glass the days would fall and rise,
I never would have felt the exquisite ache,
Of knowing I'd gladly die for that loved one's sake.

If I never had held close, a child of mine,
Who in my heart, sun's brightest beams outshine,
I would not have known such a heaven could exist,
Or known a love I was helpless to resist.

If I had never heard the wind at evening's close,
When the lamp is lit and the weary seek repose,
I would not have known where legends come to weep,
Or felt so close to God; before untroubled sleep.

The Winding Stairs

She dwelt within my heart awhile,
And then she went away,
When death grew jealous of her smile,
And would not let her stay.

And now she walks where angels walk,
Her beauty fair as theirs,
And heaven's hymns are sweeter now,
Since she climbed death's winding stairs.

I see the shining shells she sought,
By the frayed fringe of the sea,
They sparkle through my tumbling tears,
Where once she walked with me.

I fret among the fading flowers,
With nought to live for now,
And death that came too soon before,
Cares not for me somehow.

Lost

Let death come silent when I'm sleeping,
I've ceased to care how soon or late,
Let me languish where there's no more weeping,
And where oblivion's dark horizons wait.

And let my cries though sorrow shrouded,
Release me from perennial pain,
My once blue skies are grey and clouded,
In grief's grim harbour I can not remain.

My heart; my soul; are still song-haunted,
By melodies that come and go,
They torture me with thoughts unwanted,
As the tides of anguish ebb and flow.

I am lost upon a sea of longing,
No friendly light can pierce the gloom,
May some small wind come before the morning,
To stir my sails; and bring me home.

Touch A Star

Last night I saw the stars shine on the ocean,
As I sat upon a sea-moss mantled stone,
And the whispering waves weaved round my heart a notion,
That a dream-voice called me from some place unknown.

It said : "I have watched you as you sojourn in the darkness,
You seem to see things that to others are unseen,
As you sit in silence savouring the stillness,
Your countenance unclouded and serene".

Do you wonder if the wisdom of the ages,
Lies hidden on this wild weed tangled shore?
You know it won't be found by scribes or sages,
Their quest has failed too many times before.

I said: "This glorious gift is everywhere around us,
If we count our many blessings one by one,
And pray that peace and hope and harmony surrounds us,
And give thanks for each dying day; each rising sun".

This wisdom is the harvest that we gather,
When we accept how things were; and how things are,
And let "love" be our password to the future,
We will reach beyond our dreams; and touch a star.

Mahon Falls (Names Upon A Stone)

When evening glides with ghostly tread,
Across Comeragh's purple peaks,
The torrent's tongue of Mahon Falls,
In muted thunder speaks.

'Tis I that hear it still so clear,
Though a thousand leagues away,
I wonder if I went back again,
Would it be the same today?

I well recall those rugged slopes,
And the shadowed, sheltered bower,
Where memory's brush with memory's strokes,
Paint fauna, fern and flower.

Does the verdant moss cling to the stone,
As it did long, long ago?
Do the deep rock-pools still stem the stream,
Where the brown trout hide below?

Does the river rush; then stop awhile,
And gossip as it goes?
It tells it's stories to my soul,
As through my mind it flows.

I wonder if soft Comeragh winds,
Are across the hillsides heard?
And is the rainbow tinted Mahon mist,
By those sighing zephyrs stirred?

There's a secret nook by the waterfall,
That's known to me alone,
Where I stooped to etch with loving care,
Two names upon a stone.

Then I gifted them to the wind and rain,
That will their secret keep,
The ghosts that heard a whispered name,
Have been for years asleep.

I wonder if they're worn away,
Or by green moss overgrown?
Are they still washed by Mahon's tears,
Those names upon a stone?

The Flowers Of Today

We may sometimes wish today would be tomorrow,
Or yearn for some rose-tinted yesterday,
Such hopeless dreams breed discontent and sorrow,
And steals the fragrance from the flowers of today.

We cannot lure the buds break into blossom,
For everything there is a season and a date,
In God's good time all things will reach fruition,
And for that time we can only watch and wait.

Be an autumn leaf that floats upon life's river,
Unresisting to the currents that onwards flow,
And meander among the blond-tressed reeds that shiver,
In ecstasy when soft sensuous zephyrs blow.

And seek sanctuary far from the crowded pathway,
By ten thousand weary travellers trampled clean,
And turn away from the well signposted highway,
And find contentment by some misty mountain stream.

Life's Garden

Life's garden will bloom and blossom,
With our every word and thought,
With the harvests we have gathered,
And the battles we have fought.

When wild flowers fringed the headlands,
Did we offer thanks for them?
In our greed for the garden's bounty,
Did we hack them from the stem?

Did we somehow miss the message,
That was blazoned on the tree,
Where they crucified the saviour,
On the hill of Calvary?

Life's garden will bloom and blossom,
In true measures to what we've wrought,
If we plant the vines of venom,
We will reap the Grapes of Wrath.

When shadows dim the evening skies,
Will we regret the wasted hours?
In our arrogance did we allow,
The weeds to flourish with the flowers?

Deirdre

She always sat by the flickering fire,
And gazed at the dancing flames,
The clouds that filled her little mind,
Left no room for childish games.

Her cornflower eyes the sun had kissed,
And her hair like harvest sheaves,
But her smile was for someone she saw,
Who laughed among the leaves.

When her second spring came blustering in,
With burgeoning buds and showers,
With faltering steps she rose and stood,
With death among the flowers.

When evening came she slipped away,
With the sun behind the hill.
But beyond the boundaries of our grief,
She's waiting for us still.

She was ours for such a little while,
One of God's small treasures lent,
And angel hearts were sorrowing,
With wondering why she went.

They cajoled her to come back to them,
In every whispering breeze,
With tales of children dancing,
On the shores of silver seas.

The world from her concealed its charms,
Yet it sparkled when she smiled.
That was when an angel's gentle arms,
Embraced our darling child.

"O Deirdre, with the golden hair,
If only dreams came true,
To-night I'd sit beside the fire,
And sing my songs to you".

Ships That Pass In The Night

I stand on the shore in the wind and the rain,
And the moon's face is hidden in a turmoil of clouds,
I hear ships in the distance at their moorings complain,
And the screams of the wind in their shivering shrouds.

I stand with my face to the surge of the sea,
Where the torments of thunder and lightning's luminous spears,
Can scarce touch the passion my heart held for thee,
When love's nectar we drained from the goblet of years.

Spring blossomed with tokens of times not yet known,
As I traced with my fingers the blushing rose of your cheek,
Summer sang it's sweet songs with your hand in my own,
And loving words of affection we scarce needed to speak.

I have tasted the fires of love on your lips,
Did they burn too intensely in dusk's lingering light?
Now we drift down the tide like two rudderless ships,
Nor acknowledge each other when we pass in the night.

On a wintry shore in the wind and the rain,
The moon's face is hidden in the tormented skies,
And I am still tortured by love's exquisite pain,
Now there's no one to kiss the salt tears from my eyes.

The Sound Of The Sea

In the sound of the sea do I sometimes stand,
And watch the white waves weeping,
Their frothy tears on the silver strand,
As dusk o'er the day is creeping.

The turbulent tide saturates my soul,
With the harmonies of nature,
The rapture of its deep drum roll,
Is forged on my every feature.

Up the darkening dome climbs many a star,
That is mirrored on the ocean,
As the grumbling waves wash o'er the bar,
With perpetual percussive motion.

More passioned pursuits could scarce achieve,
The content that comes unbidden,
As ancestral seas advance and recede,
At the whim of a lunar rhythm,

Still I stand and stare in pensive peace,
At the night's dark cloak unfolding,
As the heavenly spheres fling their silver spears,
At the white waves around me rolling.

Dungarvan Fair

I have tasted the sweetness of memory's wine,
In the star-silvered nocturnes of night,
If the glass overflows – the fault is all mine,
It's quaint vintage I quaff with delight.

But one memory gleams in the moon's pallid glow,
And it's bouquet still hangs in the air,
'Till I'm drunk with the dreams of a lost long ago,
Driving cattle to Dungarvan Fair.

I can hear the lowing laments of the herd,
Like a banshee's wail of despair,
Reverberate in my dreams like the requiems I heard,
When we walked through the dark to the fair.

I see the gossamer veil of vaporous breath,
That hung in the haunted air,
In the shimmering starlight's silhouette,
Of the cattle we drove to the fair.

Icicles fringed the frost-frozen thatch,
And the pulse of the world was quiet,
And the frowning front doors limply leaned on the latch,
As the wind strummed the strings of the night.

When grey dawn awoke in the amorphous East,
And night's mantle was folded away,
It revealed a tableau of man, boy and beast,
Like sculptures at the gates of the day.

There we stoically stood 'till the cattle were sold,
Feigned indifference our anxiety clad,
'Till the last palm was slapped, and we garnered the gold,
Like ancient merchant sheikhs of Baghdad.

Time's Procession

As the years on one another pile up scenes of other days,
That in memories dusted mirror flare and fade,
I wait for them at twilight with distant drowsy gaze,
As one by one in times procession, before me they parade.

A young man's dreams and dramas dance about me and then go,
And scenes of sadness for which time must bear the blame,
They ignite forgotten fires in the hearths of long ago,
But there are dreams among the ashes I will never fan to flame.

I have travelled far along the road that knows no turning back,
And the faltering steps were mingled with the fair,
Though there were good days beyond number
there were days of midnight black,
That still haunt me and still hurt me in the peaceful evening air.

There is no use now regretting what might not or might have been,
And we each must plough life's furrow on our own,
With wisdom born of sorrow in all the brown days and the green,
And the time we thought eternal, that has Oh! so quickly flown.

When a veil of sweet oblivion like a dew on me will rest,
And my tired eyes will close forever more,
I will stand before my maker and say to him "I've done my best",
And he knowing human frailty will say " I never asked for more!"

How Sweet The Rose

The candle burning at both ends,
Is a self-consumer of the light,
It's brief delights a longing lends,
To the hurt that haunts my heart tonight.

Life's ruined river rushes on,
Between heart-broken banks of pain,
Of the light that on those waters shone,
Only spectral shadows still remain.

From passions past; let me repose,
In some strange place; alone; apart.
I never knew how sweet the rose,
Until it's thorn pierced my heart.

No parting kiss will fan love's fires,
No parting sigh caress a cheek,
If in sombre silence love expires,
In this agony, let the silence speak.

The Secret Door

Though the mundane mists of time define the day,
When dusk-dimmed trees are full of folding wings,
My dreams escape once more to dance and play,
From the casket where I hoard my secret things.

When midnight's hour is sliding past the moon,
In the silence I still hear a soft voice call,
And ever closer rustling footsteps coming soon,
To let my kisses on your dew-drenched eyelids fall.

When dawn lights in the East the lamps of day,
Where the silhouette of fires forever flare,
All the tangled tear-fringed memories delay,
To stir to flame the fires you kindled there.

Prized possessions are my dreams of you,
Those secret sighs that stirred the peaceful air,
When love grew wings and round about us flew,
And disturbed the lights that dance among your hair.

Then I lock the secret door that has no key,
And hide away my treasures once again,
Where no thief that stalks the night can steal from me,
My jewelled casket of exquisite pain.

The Winds Of Change

When Cupid's arrow found its mark,
Love's flame ignited from its spark,
Discordant words were as yet unheard,
Grief's cauldron was as yet unstirred.

But the winds of change did quietly blow,
You went; I did not hear you go,
The glowing torch you quenched at will,
For me, the torch is burning still.

Without a backward glance or care,
You left me broken-hearted there,
Among the tangled threads of pain,
You around me weaved with cruel disdain.

The moth that seeks the candle flame,
Seduced by the light forgets the pain,
And flings himself into the fire,
And surrenders all to a mad desire.

No Heaven More Than This...

Every breeze is scented with a sensuous joy,
And sings sweet songs where sorrow reigned supreme,
The rainbow's coloured cloak hangs in the sky,
When love's harps hang on the willows of a dream.

I will warm your hands without, and heart within,
And unencumbered by earth's chains, soar free as air,
And leave my mark upon your burning skin,
Lest sometime you might forget, when I'm not there.

My heart is overcome by mad delight,
When I walk with you down a dusk-dim whispering lane,
And day at last embraces ebony night,
And the moon's wan face is worn in the window pane.

Sated silence seduces me to sleep,
Intoxicated by the fragrance of your hair,
I will sense your warm breath upon my cheek,
No heaven more than this could be as fair.

The Power Of Love

My heart is a fountain of fervour,
That pulses with passions untold,
And soars free on the wings of the morning,
And touches the heavens with gold.

There's a joy that outreaches rapture,
In a heart inspired and filled,
With a vision that outshines all visions,
And a song that will not be stilled.

In the rose-lit regions I hear it,
As I lounge by Elysian streams,
Every hour is enriched and enchanted,
And rainbows repose in my dreams.

What power is this that enslaves me?
That's within me; about me; above;
Who's gossamer chains can't be broken,
Poets call it "The Power of Love!"

Pictures In My Mind

As the sun rests on the water, and the
evening's growing cold,
I recall delightful mornings
and remember days of gold.
When the whole world was my oyster,
and barely big enough for me,
I often watched the sunset's furnace,
burn beyond the China Sea.

And the gold and purple evenings
on the Island of Japan,
Where the silk-clad geisha's singing
would steal the soul of any man.
But the turning tide was calling and
some hypnotic strange perfume,
Send the scents of other seaports
waiting out there in the gloom.

The carousing with my shipmates in
foreign star bejewelled towns,
And the girls with blue-black tresses,
wearing rainbow coloured gowns,
And the music and the magic,
and the laughter and the sport,
And the sailors fickle fondness,
for a girl in every port.

And the myriad sounding voices
were a mystic melody,
That kept tugging at my heartstrings
and kept calling, calling me.
And the lamp-light on the water
was a rainbow in repose,
Those scenes my soul remembers,
with the tincture of the rose.

The old "Tramp-Steamers" that I sailed in,
and the shipmates that I knew,
Are quietly waiting by the quayside;
the time for leaving overdue.
Palatial liners leave their moorings
in the evening's sunset glow,
But old "Tramp-Steamers" and old sailors
populate the world I know.

And now even if I went there,
it would not be the same,
Though the sunset on the water
would still as brightly flame,
The world has turned too many times,
and it's left me far behind,
Now those perfumed ports and
places are only pictures in my mind.

Rainbow's End

When twilight hangs a halo round your hair,
Memories minstrels sing so sweet, I'm moved to weep,
And sighing in the April evening air,
Little zephyrs lull the lazy sun to sleep.

When God's taper is touched by twilight to the stars,
And hand in hand we walk in evening's gloam,
Love overfills the seasons and the years,
And evening lights the lamps to lead us home.

And contented we'll find peace at close of day,
By a warm spark-spitting fire lest we grow cold,
And in the after silence let us stay,
To repose at Rainbow's End when grey and old.

Springtime

When April sings it's songs of the morning,
I see the splendours of spring everywhere,
In scented showers are rainbows sojourning,
And the lark's overtures haunt the air.

The gaunt ghost of the wearisome winter,
Has long fled the frost-frozen stage,
And went not with a roar: but a whimper,
And scarce a remnant of it's once riotous rage,

Winter went like a lost memory – weeping,
But I heed not it's lost mournful cries,
I'm seduced by the springtime's awakening,
And the symphony of bird-song in the skies.

From the hillsides come silver streams – singing,
Over rocks and round ridges they dance,
Down dark valleys their laughter is ringing,
From the realms of re-echoes romance.

And far horizons are hazy at evening,
Scarcely seen in the gossamer gloom,
Twilight's floors; are myopic bats sweeping,
With their whispering wings as a broom.

Such delights strum my heartstrings with gladness,
When the whitethorns and whins are in bloom,
Though those blossoms are harbingers of sadness,
Spring's sweet songs will grow silent too soon.

The Bugler 1917

I learned to blow the bugle,
And blow "Revielle" at the dawn,
And "Last Post's" sad notes at sunset,
As the flag was lowered down.
But dying was never mentioned,
Or combat's cruel campaign,
Or the bodies heaping higher,
Or the reek and the rats and the rain.

Or the terror in the trenches,
As the shells screamed overhead,
When there's mud above our ankles,
Or else we're walking on the dead.
We charged the guns at daybreak,
And comrades on either hand,
Hung like my mother's washing,
On barbed wire in "No–Man's–Land".

Did no one hear my pleading,
Did no one see my pain,
As the bombs exploded round me,
Again and yet again.
I cowered in a crater,
With cruel death my chaperone,
To my neck in dirty water,
Fifteen years old; and all alone.

I never saw the star-shell,
That lit the night as day,
And I never heard the bullet,
In my lodgings in the clay.
I heard no cannon's thunder,
Nor the shrapnel overhead,
I am sleeping in a shell-hole,
In the acres of the dead.

Through pains portal's eyes are dimming,
In wars raging rant and roar,
And the dripping drops of crimson,
Turns the water red with gore.
And the twisting face that trembles,
In reflection's tortured breath,
Is for the fearful face above it,
The bewildered face of death.

Soon the poppies will be blooming,
And the groping grasses creep,
Round the bloated broken bodies,
That lately fell asleep.
I sent my wages home to mother,
Who waits beyond the sea,
Tomorrow she'll get the letter,
That will talk to her of me.

The Lady Belle

The quayside is now lonely and the seagull's cry is shrill,
And the small waves whisper to me as I pass Moloney's Mill,
And though the anchorage is crowded with boats of every kind,
It's not of them that I am dreaming; I have a "Lady" on my mind.

'Tis for the "Lady Belle" I'm longing and she sailing hard for home,
With a black south-easter screaming and her decks awash with foam,
And her bow-wave curled and creamy rushing past her midship rail,
But she rears and plunges onward as she battles through the gale.

I remember well the morning a marauding German plane,
Dropped it's dreadful bombs around us while it's
guns were spitting flame,
I still can hear the howling of the engine's eerie note,
In the tortured air above us, as though from a banshee's throat.

When his cannons were exhausted, the craven coward flew away,
And the "Belle" sailed on though crippled, and tied up at Milford Quay,
Then Tom Donoghue, the Captain, and the "Lady's" gallant crew,
Raised a toast of thanks to the bravest boat that ever water drew.

Through those years of strife and torment, when the war was
at it's height,
She dodged German mines in daylight and silent submarines at night,
At the dockside in Dungarvan she dropped her cargoes of black gold,
To keep the home fires burning; when the hearts of men were cold.

Now no more loads of lumber – no more cargoes of black gold,
Will fill to overflowing, her tightly battened hold,
She sailed out from Dungarvan for the last time long years past,
So sadly; yet so proudly; Moloney's pennant on her mast.

I'm still haunted by old memories, that disturb me day and night,
But I never more will see my "Belle", she is gone beyond my sight.
Port and starboard lights are gleaming and her mast-head light's aglow,
On that "Lady" of my longing – I loved years and years ago.

I dream I see the dancing waves still white against her prow,
I dream I see the harbour lights of ports forgotten now,
I dream I see the billows break on beach and bar and shoal,
You stole my heart, my "Lady Belle"; and maybe too my soul.

The Things I Should Have Said

In the grey tinted twilight when embers are glowing,
And dusk paints its pictures of the past on my mind,
And velvet-soft memories are coming and going,
The silence surrounds me and there's rain on the wind.

I fancy I hear footsteps fall on the threshold,
But it's only the last lingering leaves that lodge there,
And they frighten the flame of the lamp on the cupboard,
As the wind weaves the wreathes that winter will wear.

Time seems so short since spring greened the pastures,
And the house rang with singing and children at play,
Too work-worn and weary to rejoice in their raptures,
The song died on their lips when I pushed them away.

Those faces I loved that looked so bewildered,
Haunt me tonight in the embers soft glow,
From daybreak to dark, I toiled and I laboured,
But it's scant consolation when the tears start to flow.

Like the swallows in summer they have roamed the world over,
Blown hither and yon on the wings of the air,
I was unfair and foolish, but they mention it never,
And the post-script "love always" makes it harder to bear.

The ghosts of regret have now gathered round me,
If I could only unravel times tangled thread,
And show them I loved them so softly, so gently,
And at last say the things I should have long ago said.

The Tides Of Time

On this tide and time there flows a quiet reflection,
That laps the shores of sorrow and delight,
Thoughts of those I love are the blooms of my affection,
And for those I've lost, I grow grey with grief tonight.

The morning sun brought love and joy and laughter,
But I grow weary, weak and wan at it's demise,
Now with shorter steps days follow each one after,
And with shorn wings, I reach no more for the skies,

When dusk obscures the drowsy eyes of evening,
And the dead leaves of regret replace my dreams,
I watch the ribbons of remorse around me weaving,
Like seaweed fronds in turbulent tidal streams.

Infinity thrives on secrecy and silence,
While the finite can scarce forget the here and now,
It matters not how we embrace youth's eager essence,
We are shackled to what span life will allow.

Twenty One

The young years slipped from my embrace,
When apple orchards dimmed the skies,
Winter weaved too soon it's sombre lace,
To close the curtains of my eyes.

Life sang for me too short a while,
Now the singer's lips are nearly dumb,
Signposts of pain mark every mile,
And clouds pile up behind the sun.

Gone are the yearning carefree years,
Like storm-blown smoke they are no more,
The rain obscures my falling tears,
The wind wails round the closing door.

Dawn cloaked me in a gown of gold,
With the kiss of morning on my mouth,
Now evening's whispering wings unfold,
As the lingering lamps of day go out.

I can see the sun's last latticed hue,
Illumine my path with suffused light,
Where waits the final rendezvous,
In the pallid pastures of the night.

Now evening calls the last bird home,
With requiems for the day that's spent,
And death demands in the gathering gloom,
Recompense for twenty-one years lent.

The Wreaths Of December

We gather the fruits of our summertime days,
When the acolytes of autumn softly sing in the fields,
As the winnowing wind on the ripe harvest plays,
And reawakens the splendour of dreams unrevealed.

But many a dream will have withered and died,
And the petals will have blown from the rose,
Now the heart only hears in the silence inside,
The wings of life's melody close.

On the wall was the writing there plain to be seen,
From the seeds we have sown we remember,
And from buds that have blossomed in spring's emerald green,
We have fashioned the wreaths of December.

Faugheen Chapel

The shadows hide behind the golden sheaves,
Where the "sallies" shyly kiss the crystal stream,
And the slanting sun shows the webs the spider weaves,
Like silk cartwheels round the church door in Faugheen.

Where windows face the west a fire gleams,
As though heaven's light was shining from within,
Alas; 'tis but the twilight's stray sunbeams,
Still I hear the angels whispering in the wind.

Down the dusty road where long forgotten feet,
Came to worship faithfully at Sunday mass,
The curlew's plaintive cry their prayers repeat,
In faint echoes to the emerald graveyard grass.

Here I sit in pensive silence for a while,
Where furze wasp-yellow, frame the fields with gold,
Upon the worn well remembered stile,
Where I used to sit ere the world and I grew old.

As the golden looms of memory weave their spell,
Around the silent passing pageant of the years,
From "Saleen" I hear the mournful evening bell,
And the wild waves wash Bonmahon with their tears.

I'm heart-haunted by the Copper Coast's green shore,
Where leaning into legend I can dream,
And see again fond friends I'll see no more,
Who sleep at peace beside the chapel in Faugheen.

Now the darkness spreads it's dim star-spangled shawl,
And silence reigns supreme on sea and land,
A white-faced moon leans on the graveyard wall,
And blesses those below with pallid hand.

Sallies = Willows

Believe In Yourself

When the high tides of hope from the shoreline recedes,
Don't turn away with a sigh of despair,
But believe in yourself and you are sure to succeed,
Life's abundance of treasures to share.

If you think you are beaten, you won't stand a chance,
Don't entertain the least thought you may fail,
But reach for the stars and with courage advance,
And against all the odds you'll prevail.

If you don't deviate from the dreams that you crave,
You will find every door has a key,
If you believe in yourself and always be brave,
You'll surpass all you thought you could be.

All Is Well

Evening's drapes are hanging from the heavens,
And dusk is camped beside the dimming door,
The probing furtive fingers of the twilight,
Steal silently across the kitchen floor.

The reaper's scythe is silent in the meadow,
The fisherman is tired of the tide;
The children are around the fireside gathered,
The leaning latch has locked the world outside.

The tree-tops in the grove are softly sighing,
Their trembling twigs in anxiety intertwined,
As they await the sensuous kiss of rain; their lover,
And tonight the rain is whispering in the wind.

And aged hearts within the white-walled cabins,
Find affinity with hearts forever young,
When phantoms of the past at dusk awaken,
Illusions of a time long past and gone.

The flickering lamps are flowering on the hillside,
Across the heather tolls the evening bell,
The shadows stretch along the peaceful pastures,
The moon climbs the hills of heaven; all is well.

Laugh Or Weep

There is no door that has no key,
And no road that has no bend,
Or a soul that has no sanctuary,
Or a journey that has no end.

There is no heart that knows no pain,
No labour that knows no ease,
Or an azure sky that knows no rain,
Or a passion you can't appease.

There is no echo that won't resonate,
Though the voice does not remain,
There is no silence that does not wait,
For the laughter to peal again.

There is no seed that you will sow,
But it's harvest you will one day reap,
Whether it be flowers or weeds that grow,
Will decide if you laugh or weep.

Silent Night

As I stood in the stygian darkness,
One Christmas midnight alone,
I searched for the face of the Saviour,
In celestial realms unknown.

But the night was sombre and silent,
As though the pulse of the world had ceased,
And earth was as one with the heavens,
But for one shining star in the East.

Then the breath of a breeze from the ocean,
Brought the scent of a far-away sea,
And stirred in my heart an emotion,
That the Saviour was listening to me.

Then the divine lamplighter of Heaven,
Fanned to flame the dark dome of the sky,
Though his face in the stars was still hidden,
I knew the Redeemer was nigh.

The Helping Hand

Is there someone who will stretch a hand,
Across life's troubled waters,
To the overburdened underdog,
Who stumbles, falls and falter?

Is there someone who will help lost ones,
To find what they are seeking?
Who will soothe the fears and dry the tears,
Of faces wet with weeping?

Who will light a lamp in someone's soul,
That is in darkness shaded,
And round him drape dawn's coloured cloak,
When the fears of night have faded.

One who will ease a stranger's pain,
When the clouds of grief have gathered,
And delay the dark for a little while,
When love's light is by heartache shadowed.

Who will not want your worldly praise,
Or reward for service rendered,
But will fan to flame your dreams again,
When such dreams are scarce remembered.

Yet the helping hand may only be,
One draught from hope's clear fountain,
That will turn tired eyes to the golden skies,
That shine beyond grief's mountain.

The Gods Of Long Ago

The old Gods that once we cherished: do they still hold sway?
Over who we are, or who we might have been?
Or are they just foolish phantoms like
childish treasures thrown away,
Lost forever and forgotten by the dreamer and the dream?

Are they dishonoured outcasts in this ruthless world of greed,
That meander through the moonscapes of the mind?
Are we now so self-sufficient that Gods help we do not need?
Or does the heart search in the silence for the olden ways to find?

Have we forgotten how to love? Have we forgotten how to care?
Have we forgotten how to lend a helping hand?
Is the God we call compassion in our hearts no longer there?
And are our treasured crystal mansions built on sand?

When melodeons and moonlight mingled, and the fiddle
    sobbed its song,
And you could lift the latch on every neighbour's door,
And though piety and poverty seared the souls of weak and strong,
'Twas a gentler world when we knew the Gods of yore.

A Million Miles Away

Does the corncrake's raucous cry still ring?
Is the cuckoo's note heard yet?
Do potato flowers the furrows fill,
In the fields I can't forget?

Have they saved the hay on Helvick's Hill,
In these dying days of June?
Do the ricks rise up in silhouette,
Piled high against the moon?

Are the oat-fields patched with poppy flowers?
Do the ghostly moonbeams stray,
Among the myriad mackerel shoals,
That splinter the crystal bay?

But I was banished from those scenes,
And from a daughter's name,
The heart that beat beneath my heart,
Was the harvest of my shame.

My shame was that I loved too much,
Eyes stared like levelled guns,
Did they not see I shared the blame,
With their unsullied sons?

I believed the breathless, languorous lies,
Were a rose without a thorn,
How could I know love's fervid fires,
Would be ashes in the morn?

It seems like a thousand years ago,
And sometimes like yesterday,
Since I gazed across at Helvick's Hill,
A million miles away.

Elizabethan Serenade

Around me, the shadows were stretching,
My heart throbbed with a troubled disquiet,
In the lonely labyrinthine alleys,
Of a mist shrouded city at night.

From the depths of a dim dismal doorway,
Where a home for the night she had made,
A pallid faced girl with a mandolin,
Played "Elizabethan Serenade".

She succumbed to the spell of the music,
And her pain she poured into the tune,
'Till the notes from her flickering fingers,
Round her feet like rose petals were strewn.

And the sounds so sad and so soothing,
Threw a noose round the ebb-tides of time,
'Till the darkness seemed sprinkled with stardust,
And my cheeks with the soft salt sea rime.

It surged like a wave swirling round me,
And I was carried away on it's crest,
To a long ago time and a far-away place,
As a swallow flies home to it's nest.

A sigh down the darkness went stumbling,
To where the willows weaved a mantle of shade,
And a girl who softly sang in the sunset,
"Elizabethan Serenade".

An angel's chorus then merged with the music,
And night filled with the scent of the glade,
And a voice from a long ago evening,
Sang "Elizabethan Serenade".

The Ribbons Of Day

In the solace and silence of twilight,
Let me turn time's torn pages of old,
Let me wander through youth's mystic meadows,
And childhood's glorious gardens of gold.

May melancholy retreat to the shadows,
When the ribbons of day are drawn tight,
May the wayward wild winds of imagination,
Blow through my mind's mansions tonight.

Let me dream forgotten dreams of past ages,
Let fancy spread wide wings and take flight,
An may memories undisturbed in dark dungeons,
Break from bondage and dance round me tonight.

May I meet with old friends and old lovers,
Let us share songs and stories once more,
On ancestral avenues of innocence,
Let waves of wonder break again on youth's shore.

Thy Will Be Done

Often good intentions exceed good deeds!
Where there's human frailty and earthly needs.
I try my best; but so often fall,
That I sometimes wonder if I'll rise at all.

When shadows fall across the heart,
And from God's great goodness I drift apart,
But he will not turn his face away,
He knows I'm weak; He knows I stray;

When death will come and dim my eyes,
He will reach for my hand, from beyond the skies,
"Lord! I am your child! I am your son!
I did my best! Thy will be done!"

The Sinner

Is compassion just a glib word we utter?
Do we treat he who falls with disdain?
Do we help him struggle up from the gutter?
Or do we just watch him struggle in vain?

Shame's brush-strokes are not daubed by another,
But by our failure to stand up for what's right,
And not forgive our less fortunate brother,
And turn our eyes from his pitiful plight.

Must he forever bear the scars of misfortune,
Though for his failings he tries to atone,
And be subjected to scorn and suspicion,
By those least worthy to cast the first stone.

Can there never be hope for the sinner,
Though he may purge his soul of it's guilt?
Is not he who repents a true winner?
On such as he were great kingdoms once built?

May our forgiveness be a draught of cool water,
In the searing desert sun of his pain,
And from the ashes of alienation's cruel crater,
May he rise like a phoenix again.

The Song Of The Scythe

The scythe hangs from the cow-shed's shadowed rafters,
It's once burnished blade now dulled to russet red,
The spider weaves his web round the well-worn handles,
Uncaring of harvests reaped by hands long dead.

The dew-damp dawn shone on it's shearing sharpness,
As the honing-stone seduced the singing steel,
To a razor's edge with rhythmic careful cadence,
As the golden glow of morning filled the field.

And bent like half a heart from clamp to handle,
A "sallee" stretched the swaths in serried lines,
With each unhurried stroke precisely measured,
By a reaper reaching back to bygone times.

In my heart I hear again the morning chorus,
Where the harvest fields are stirring like the sea,
And the scythe is singing in the bearded barley,
A serenade to mark the season's rosary.

Those lovely childhood days have now long left us,
And fallow lie the fields where waved the corn,
The reaper set the scythe upon the rafters,
And to reap his heavenly harvest now has gone.

"Sallee" – *A flexible willow-wand fixed to the scythe tree to guide the falling corn in a straight line.*

Tomorrow

Sometimes we fail though we have tried our best,
By the width of a thumb-nail narrow,
But do not fret, it's not over yet,
We will try again tomorrow.

'Tis the way of the world that we win or lose,
As we plough a lonely furrow,
Though courage fails; confront life's gales,
And pray for tranquil seas tomorrow.

Sometimes we dance and sometimes we sing,
And sometimes we're wracked with sorrow,
But don't forget there's a long road yet,
And let hope fill your heart tomorrow.

Though the night is dark and we've lost our way,
And we can neither lead 'nor follow,
But have no fear the dawn is near,
And the sun will shine tomorrow.

The Underdog

He's the man who will labour from morning 'till night,
And at life's end merit no epilogue,
He will drift through the days just a face in the crowd,
And always the underdog.

He's the flotsam that floats on the ocean of life,
Half submerged like a tempest-tossed log,
At the whim of the wave and the will of the wind,
A browbeaten underdog.

This insignificant soul will go unrecognised,
Though through shine and shadow he'll slog,
An bear every burden that's heaped on his back,
And be forever the underdog.

When "High Kings" of commerce display avarice and greed,
Of such magnitude it leaves us agog,
On them justice bestows a benevolent smile,
But it frowns on the underdog.

And when things go wrong, he's the one they will blame,
And his long list of faults catalogue,
While the fat cats still bury their face in the cream.
And to hell! With the underdog.

The Wage Slave

We travel the well-worn winding track,
That the weary wage-slaves blaze,
With calloused hands and bended back,
In life's twisted labyrinthine maze.

No nation or flag can on us lay claim,
We are not of one colour or race,
Thought different; still, we are all the same,
Nor owe allegiance to one class or place.

We are locked in labour's lecherous embrace,
Until a line through the day is drawn,
And emerge from the gloom with fungus-white face,
And re-enter again with the dawn.

It seems hardly fair, when the day is done,
The reaper will neither care or know,
Of the golden sheaves in the evening sun,
The price we paid – or the debt they owe.

Shakespeare said, "All the world's a stage!
And we each must play many parts,
Where we enter and exit from age to age,
Until the actor … from the stage departs".

In Hospital

The subdued panic; and sameness of the days,
The darkness held at bay by diffused light,
The instruments of pain in shining trays,
The snores and moans and groans that stalk the night.

In this ward I lie, a bruised and broken thing,
Where hope is hard to hold when evening falls,
And dawn another desolate day will bring,
And shadows that I watch walk down the walls.

I pray somehow that I might stronger be,
And not succumb to the depths of dark despair,
Though a light at tunnel's end I try to see,
It flickers faint; then it's no longer there.

And still I strive and hope; and still I pray,
To leave at last this death-dominioned place,
And see white sails imprinted on the bay,
And feel the suns of home fall soft upon my face.

But from my mind I never will erase,
The ministrations of kind angels dressed in white,
Through the curtains of their care I see God's face,
And hear his voice beyond the borders of the night.

The Seeds Of Sorrow

Tonight my peace is troubled,
By ghosts I can't ignore,
A voice half-heard in the darkness,
A footfall faint at the door.
A sigh that stirs the silence,
Of secret ethereal things,
That drift through the soul's dark dungeons,
With the murmur of whispering wings.

In a room consumed by shadows,
I find the secret source,
Of regrets remorseless river,
As recollection charts it's course.
When a kind word was unspoken,
When a frown replaced a smile,
When a wanderer on life's journey,
Walked alone the last long mile.

The spirit of things remembered,
The spirit of things unseen,
Like phantoms, they hover 'round me,
Unalterable and serene.
But they ransack the soul's recesses,
Where secrets and sin reside,
Till the heart is haunted by anguish,
From which it cannot hide.

Have I planted the seeds of sorrow,
With the sharp-edged tools of pain?
Have I hurt those I hold dearest,
Though their hearts still true remain?
If fond friends I have forsaken,
And darker pathways trod!
Tonight: I beg forgiveness,
From them: and from my God.

Dance With Your Daydreams

When you sit by the fire at the end of the day,
Let your thoughts like the swallows take flight,
Unfettered they'll soar to scenes far away,
Where they'll dance with your day-dreams tonight.

And the neighbours and comrades you knew long ago,
Who with you often shared half their own,
Their faces you'll see in the flame's ruddy glow,
Though long absent from around the hearthstone.

You will hear in the wind sweet songs you once knew,
And the poems that you used to recite,
And loves you had lost will whisper softly anew,
When you dance with your day-dreams tonight.

And away in the distance in silence sublime,
Lurk the ghosts of the wind and the rain,
Faint phantoms of storms on the seascapes of time,
Re-echo life's passions and pain.

You'll once more kiss the lips of sweetheart or bride,
And hold her close to you heart with delight,
And you'll feel as you felt when she stood by your side,
When you dance with your day-dreams tonight.

You will walk on the margins of musical streams,
As the moon spreads it's diamond starred cloak,
Memory's flowers will bloom in the silver-hue'd beams,
And past dreams and past passions evoke.

As the ghosts of the past gather round you again,
The grey ashes of spring will ignite,
To lure you away from dark winter's domain,
When you dance with your day-dreams tonight.

On the ocean of life you set sail with the dawn,
While the wind and the waves were asleep,
Now you're far from the shore, but you sail on and on,
A rendezvous with other day-dreams to keep.

Cloud-Shadows

Cruel fate confines my soul in chains,
My spirits gaze through prison bars,
I search through dim and dark domains,
For one clear pathway to the stars.

Summer sang in me a little while,
Then winter stole it's songs away,
Now the road is weary; every mile,
And cloud-shadows darken every day.

But the hurting heart is hidden well,
Behind a camouflage of joy,
From the clown's visage no one can tell,
Hope briefly halts; then hurries by.

Love's blossoms now I cannot find,
They have decayed, and days grow cold,
Still they strum the harpstrings of my mind,
And my heart their ghostly arms enfold.

Is there some secret sun-soaked shore,
Beyond the vast and surging seas,
Where a hopeless heart will weep no more,
And a troubled mind might be at ease?

Beyond The Stars

Keep your spirits strong – let it not be broken,
By the twin-pronged spear of penury and pain,
Meet a wilderness of woe with distress unspoken,
And believe the sun comes always after rain.

Though fate may hurl your hopes upon the ebb-tide,
And your spirit be restrained by prison bars,
Let your mind fly free to the farthest, highest hillside,
And let your soul soar somewhere far beyond the stars.

While the sun's last rays to the clouds torn cloaks are clinging,
Take sensuous ease beside some slumbering stream,
And listen to the sonorous sighs of evening,
In the silver tinted twilight drowse and dream.

Contented may you rest when day is ended,
When there is no more time to worry; or to weep,
And may peace be yours when day with night is blended,
In the hush when you succumb to dreamless sleep.

Ardmore

I lean upon an old stone wall at sunset,
On a hill above the village of Ardmore,
As the azure skies turn russet red around me,
Creeping shadows steal the gold from Curragh's shore.

And drowsy, dreamy memories are dancing,
To childhood's charming tunes of long ago,
When I thought Saint Declan's Tower touched the heavens,
Like a stairway to the stars for folks below.

And in winter's wrath the wild wave's foamy fingers,
Encroached beyond our barred and bolted door,
Along the cliff road little houses shook and shivered,
When raucous south-east storms roared round Ardmore.

In the quiet I hear again the mournful murmurs,
And the anguished cries that haunt me evermore,
When some little boat did not come home at sunset,
And some mother's son lies dead on the dim sea-floor.

But peace pervades Ardmore this autumn evening,
In Ballyquin I watch the cows meander home,
The moon peeps o'er the shoulder of Goat Island,
And I can hear the small waves whispering in the gloam.

I've been enchanted by these village streets since childhood,
By this hallowed wave-washed hamlet I've been blessed,
When the benediction of final darkness falls upon me,
Beneath Ardmore's green grass; I'll gladly rest.

And Then ...

Melancholy's morose miasma,
Indistinct and undefined,
In vague atmospheres of anguish,
Swirled unfettered through my mind.

Then a friend rushed up to greet me,
His countenance creased with joy,
At such unexpected pleasure,
To see me passing by.

Immersed in the mists of misery,
No kind words had I to give,
To the faithful heart that would find no fault,
But forget and forever forgive.

His presence to flame stirred the embers,
In the ashes of despair,
And friendship's breath dispersed the clouds,
And a heaven was still there.

One friend that's true is beyond all wealth,
That fortune's wheel might bring,
Who will take your world of winter,
And give back a world of spring.

I have been blessed with such a friend,
Whose love will never fail,
He holds my heart through light and dark,
And then; he wags his tail.

Beyond Hope's Broken Beacons

For the worthless wasteland of my life,
The blame is but my own,
And the trailing threads on the gowns of grief,
Were weaved by me alone.

I'm the architect of all my woes,
The master of my misery,
I'm crucified on life's cruel cross,
And the nails were hammered home by me.

I'm beyond hope's broken beacons,
Where the lamplights all are quenched,
And the winds of woe are howling,
And the road to hell unfenced.

I smothered the flames that flickered,
In the burnt-out fires of youth,
I trampled the petals of promise,
Lies shattered the shrines of truth.

I walk as one who is dreaming,
And careless am I of change,
I note not the dawn or darkness,
'Nor the commonplace or strange.

Is there some sanctuary of solace,
Or some refuge from distress,
Where sleep's soft embrace is waiting,
And sweet forgetfulness?

Is there perhaps a tranquil haven,
And a road without a bend,
Someplace to rest at sunset,
And peace at journey's end?

Life I know is a game of chance,
With forlorn hopes of winning,
Pray heaven may be kind to one,
More sinned against than sinning.

Noreen
(To The Memory Of Noreen Egan, Who Died Tragically In Australia)

Since you unfurled your wings and left me,
I have grown gaunt eyed and grey,
From searching hurt's hostile horizons,
And hope's harbours of yesterday.

Elusive and silent as a shadow,
You slipped from my eclectic embrace,
And time painted an old man's portrait,
On the canvas of a father's face.

Somewhere, somehow, did I fail you?
I know love can be sometimes blind,
Now in temples of torment I worship,
While your footprints weave paths through my mind.

The sweet fragrance has fled from the flowers,
Since the oil in life's lamp ceased to flow,
When you vanished in the mist and the moonlight,
And I did not hear you go.

I searched to the ends of creation,
I sought you beyond crystal seas,
And grief grew in the green groves of silence,
In soft music and sweet memories.

Now the past has lost all it's lustre,
It's radiance replaced by regret,
As soft Australian winds sob around you,
"O Noreen!" How could I forget?

You brought me bouquets of the springtime,
But the petals now bleed from the rose,
When my heart hears your songs in the silence,
While the wings of the melodies close.

At Mass In Garranbane

The priest bowed down before God's holy altar,
At Sunday mass; that we might witness there,
The bread and wine to the Saviour's presence alter,
As the slanting sun lit faces flushed with prayer.

Prayer that harboured hopes for those beyond the ocean,
And for the blessings of fond friends who stayed at home,
And the wayward child for whom love's deep devotion,
In a mother's heart was a constant undertone.

Gaunt-faced men who were worn wan with labour,
And hardships that had too soon made them old,
Bent furrowed brows, and gave homage to the Saviour,
For Springtime's blooms and Autumn's gifts of gold.

And when the dew-drops strung upon the bramble,
A necklace to drape around the throat of day,
The chapel bell sent the message – "mass is ended",
And Father Roche then blessed us on our way.

Then down the furze-fringed hill we ambled slowly,
And kept a wary eye on Carroll's quick-stepping mare,
As Minnie Higgins sedately steered her old "High Nellie",
Through the heedless high-heeled Hogans… with a frosty stare.

The latest news was absorbed in wide-eyed wonder,
And old stories blossomed once again anew,
Who went away; and left fond hearts torn asunder,
And who was sick; but God willing would pull through.

There was magic in those Summer Sunday mornings,
That from memory's silken spool weaves a golden glow,
Garranbane was a jewel in the crown of childhood,
Coming home from mass: a million years ago.

Easter Week 1916

When the church bells of Easter were ringing,
In secret, men marched through the morn,
Old Fenians in old graveyards were singing,
And Yeat's "Terrible Beauty" was born.

They came from the mean streets of the city,
And down from the hungry hill farms,
Their small boats were tied fast to the jetty,
They came; when Ireland called them to arms.

They came from the mountains of Munster,
They came from Connaught's stone walls,
They came from the green glens of Ulster,
And from Leinster they answered the call.

And the schoolroom was left unattended,
The "master" had shouldered the gun,
On those rebels our freedom depended,
And every one was a hero unsung.

The poet lit a fire with his verses,
And hung his songs on the plough and the stars,
And old patriots marched past with old curses,
That consoled them in long ago wars.

But alas they marched only in hundreds,
To challenge an empire's great might,
The invader had guns beyond numbers,
And the rebels were fixed in their sight.

But undaunted they dreamed of the dawning,
When their land would at long last be free,
And the pallid-faced moon of the morning,
Would sleep in an emerald sea.

Easter Monday's sleepy silence was shattered,
By a rebel rifles stuttering roar,
And red blood on the mean streets was spattered,
By four "Lancers" whose lives were no more.

O'er the roof of the General Post Office,
The Tricolour was proudly unfurled,
Though soon obscured by the black smoke of battle,
'Twas a beacon all over the world.

For a week the war raged unabated,
With carnage and killing and pain,
And screaming shells with blood lust unsated,
Fell among them again and again.

They fought; till they could fight no longer,
And the rifles could no longer speak,
But freedom's flickering flame had grown stronger,
In that glorious; blood-soaked; Easter week.

As the buildings were burning around them,
They at last lay their guns on the ground,
And bloodied but unbowed in the mayhem,
It seemed the Fenians of old gathered round.

Though the guts of their guns ached with hunger,
Their pride would allow no retreat.
Pearse signalled they could fight on no longer,
And surrendered, in glorious defeat.

Within the tear-tarnished walls of Kilmainham,
Was sentence on those patriots preferred,
In the dusk 'ere the dawn they condemned them,
To be shot in the stonebreaker's yard.

Their last lines were to loved one and parent,
'Ere their souls soared among the bright stars,
And the fields of their dreams flowered as fragrant,
Though they blossomed behind prison bars.

Old Tom Clarke and young Thomas McDonagh,
With dignity faced death with a smile.
Patrick Pearse who walked the roads of Connemara,
Walked with them that last lonely mile.

Daly died with O'Hanrahan and Plunkett,
Who to fight from his sick bed arose.
'Ere death called him, he married his sweetheart,
And saw the Saviour's red blood on the rose.

Willie Pearse, Eamonn Ceannt and Con Colbert,
Heard the rifle's rabid raucous refrain,
And the music of that terrible concert,
Played as Mallin and Heuston were slain.

The guns barked at Tom Kent and McDermot,
As they lived; defiant they died,
And without; the benefit of a blindfold,
The firing squad shot John McBride.

They brought Connolly in on a stretcher,
And just inside the great doors shot him there,
When his wounds would not allow him go further,
They executed him strapped to a chair.

Roger Casement was charged with high treason,
And they hanged him in Pentonville Jail.
He gave his life for the cause he believed in,
May the cause he believed in prevail.

The poet's pen has at last written "Finis",
To Easter of Nineteen Sixteen,
'Oer the graves of our heroes who perished,
Still blooms the red rose of their dream.

The Shepherd

Across misty mountain moorlands with measured tread and slow,
Where rain and rainbow mingle towards cloud-piercing peaks he'll go.
Birds curve their throats to greet him with sweet springtime serenades,
And the shepherd's heart rejoices in the songbird's accolades.

Over turf that whispers wetly and thorn-tangled paths he'll plod,
'Til he scales the mountain's shoulder close to the House of God.
There he rests on a rocky outcrop, at peace above the pines,
Where the regal ridges 'round him in rugged splendour shines.

From the yearning slopes of yesteryears, a stream of memories run.
As visions vague and evanescent are by shifting shadows spun.
High above these lofty summits perhaps a loved one watches yet,
In the mountain mist that's falling, his dew-drenched eyes are wet.

The hawk at the Gates of Heaven, the owl with staring eyes,
The badger shuffling from his set, the new-born lamb's first cries,
The hare that flees with five yard leaps, the leveret and the doe,
And the sly old fox enthrals him still, as they did long long ago.

He comforts the ewe that moans in birth, lest harm should lurk unseen,
Among the purple heathered hills and the bog lands wet and green.
But a scream torments the twilight, towards the pearl-pale
    slumbering sun,
In watching well the ninety-nine; he must mourn the loss of one.